Child of Steens Mo

Child of Steens Mountain

✛

Eileen O'Keeffe McVicker

with Barbara J. Scot

OREGON STATE UNIVERSITY PRESS
CORVALLIS

Photographs courtesy of Eileen O'Keeffe McVicker

The paper in this book meets the guidelines for permanence and durability of the Committee on Production Guidelines for Book Longevity of the Council on Library Resources and the minimum requirements of the American National Standard for Permanence of Paper for Printed Library Materials Z39.48-1984.

Library of Congress Cataloging-in-Publication Data
McVicker, Eileen O'Keeffe, 1927-
  Child of Steens Mountain / Eileen O'Keeffe McVicker with Barbara J. Scot; foreword by Richard W. Etulain.
    p. cm.
  ISBN 978-0-87071-297-5 (alk. paper)
  1. McVicker, Eileen O'Keeffe, 1927—Childhood and youth. 2. McVicker, Eileen O'Keeffe, 1927—Family. 3. Steens Mountain (Or.)—Social life and customs. 4. Country life—Oregon—Steens Mountain. 5. Outdoor life—Oregon—Steens Mountain. 6. Sheep ranchers—Oregon—Steens Mountain—Biography. 7. Irish Americans—Oregon—Steens Mountain—Biography. 8. Steens Mountain (Or.)--Biography. I. Scot, Barbara J., 1942- II. Title.
  F882.H37M38 2008
  979.5'95--dc22

                          2008021138

First published in 2008 by Oregon State University Press
Printed in the United States of America

 Oregon State University Press
121 The Valley Library
Corvallis OR 97331-4501
541-737-3166 • fax 541-737-3170
http://oregonstate.edu/dept/press

I dedicate this book to my mom and dad, for without them it surely would not have happened.

My mother, Izola Ausmus-O'Keeffe
My father, Benjamin Joseph O'Keeffe

✣

Contents

Foreword

Richard W. Etulain

STAND AT THE LOWER TIP of Steens Mountain in southeastern Oregon and gaze south toward the Nevada border in the distance. Directly ahead lie the Pueblo Mountains stretching toward the horizon. To the west looms the southern end of the Catlow Rim. On the east across a slight ridge, one glimpses the vast, brown expanses of the Alvord Desert. Nearly five miles to the south and east and barely out of sight is the hamlet of Fields, a handful of scattered buildings. Turn about and look up the spine of Steens Mountain, rising precipitously to the north, the most looming presence of southeastern Oregon.

Into this bowl of space, virtually surrounded by mountain ridges and rims, came the homesteading Benjamin and (Nancy) Izola O'Keeffe family in 1930. For the next dozen years their dreams and disappointments were rooted to their 160 acres, encircled by this spare, eye-stretching landscape. From this scene and the dramatic interplay of place and people flows the girlhood story of Eileen O'Keeffe, retold here efficiently and appealingly in the pages that follow. Although the O'Keeffes may have been unaware of much of its history, the Steens Mountain area had been defining itself as an evolving space through centuries of time, a storied place that would obviously shape the lives of these newcomers. The unfolding story of this space and place, and how they came to be, needs brief retelling.

Geologists estimate that major parts of the Steens Mountain area formed more than fifteen million years in the past. During the Miocene Era, stretching from twenty-four to five million years ago, massive eruptions of lava disrupted, reformed, and rearranged ancient Oregon landscapes. In southeastern Oregon, as elsewhere in the Pacific Northwest, explosive volcanic upthrusts established the foundations of the Steens, on which later eruptions piled the gigantic basaltic formations that characterize portions of the Basin and Range area of southeastern Oregon. These rocky contours are similar to those found scattered east across the Snake River Plain of Idaho and in parts of the Pueblo Mountains stretching toward modern-day Nevada.

Thousands of years later in the Pleistocene, or Ice, Age, dramatic landscape transformations continued. Cooling conditions and expanding icecaps, beginning two to three million years in the past and lasting until eight to ten thousand years ago, gave birth to and nourished large glaciers, expanding and receding over time. In the Steens area these huge glaciers carved out U-shaped valleys on the western slopes of the mountain, such as the Big Indian Gorge, Little Blitzen Gorge, and Kiger Gorge. Archaeological remains suggest that camels, early types of horses, and large sheep lived in the area.

The first humans probably took residence in the Pacific Northwest ten to fifteen thousand years in the past. As glaciers of the Ice Age receded from mountain areas, nearby lakes began to fill, and valleys and meadows appeared. The Pleistocene era was ending, and the Holocene—the geologic era in which we live—commencing. Although archaeologists, like good scholarly debaters, contest nearly every point, most agree that the oldest evidence of humans in Oregon (about nine to ten thousand years ago) is that found in the Fort Rock area, west and a bit north of Steens Mountain. These earliest inhabitants, ancestors of later Indian groups, were hunters and gatherers living on the plants they found growing, especially near adjacent lakes, and small game animals such as rabbits. The Basin and Range areas surrounding Steens Mountain were largely arid or semiarid, but the presence of dry beds indicates that at one time the area was dotted with sizeable lakes.

Centuries later, in the early nineteenth century, visitors from Lewis and Clark (1804–6) to the first overlanders in the 1840s came to Oregon from the east, but nearly all bypassed the southeastern quadrant of the state. Explorers, missionaries, and the wagon trains down the Oregon Trail traveled on or along the Columbia River or through other parts of the northern and northwestern parts of Oregon. A few trappers working for the Hudson's Bay Company at Fort Vancouver, breakaway overlanders searching for an alternative route through central Oregon, or military expeditions ventured through or near the Steens Mountain country, but it remained Indian country. One historian asserts that not one white person permanently resided in southeastern Oregon in 1860.

The first groups of non-Indian settlers into eastern Oregon began arriving in the late 1860s. They came to join the mining booms in the region, the influx of ranchers moving north from California, and the trickle of subsistence agriculturists from the Willamette Valley searching for newer farming opportunities. Between the 1860s and the 1880s, a quick succession of gold discoveries, the removal of the Northern Paiutes by the military, and the arrival of the California cattle barons and their mushrooming herds transformed Harney County, especially areas to the west of Steens Mountain. Not surprisingly this influx of newcomers brought competitions and rapid change.

Once miners and other settlers began to spill into eastern Oregon, they quickly called upon the frontier military to clear the area of Indians. In a series of battles in the 1860s and 1870s known as the Snake Wars, the U.S. army subdued the resident Native American bands, principally Northern Paiutes (Wada Tika) and their allies. Lacking the military strength of the more militant tribes of the Plains and Northern Rockies, the Wada Tika were forced from their homelands and retreated to a vaguely defined Malheur Reservation. But when a few of the Paiutes took part in the Bannock War of 1878, that activity—combined with mounting animosity from Oregonians coveting their lands—led to the reservation being dissolved and opened to settlement. (Later, small Paiute reservations were established near Fort McDermitt on the Oregon-Nevada border and, even later, close to Burns, Oregon.) It was during this period of military pursuit of Indians that Harney County was named for Gen. William S. Harney and the name of Enoch Steen, another soldier, placed on Steens Mountain.

Once California began to place restrictions on grazing areas in northern parts of the state, cattleman looked to Oregon for newer, unrestricted rangelands. From the late 1860s into the 1890s cattle herds surged into southeastern Oregon, introducing more and more animals each year. Cattle raisers seemed convinced there would always be enough water and grass for them all. By 1900 as many as one hundred fifty thousand cattle and more than four hundred thousand sheep sprawled over Harney and Malheur county to the east. One government official investigating the number of grazing animals in the Steens Mountain area in 1901 estimated that more than seventy bands of sheep, averaging about twenty-five hundred head per band, were ranging there. That meant nearly five hundred sheep per square mile were crowding into the area for four months of summer grazing.

Not unexpectedly, these competitions led to dramatic conflicts. Indeed, the arrival of the cattle kings in the decade following the early 1870s would lead eventually to explosive confrontations by the late 1880s. Peter French starred in this story of competition and turmoil. In 1872, French trailed twelve hundred cattle belonging to him and his boss, Dr. Hugh James Glenn (later French's father-in-law) of California, into the Blitzen River basin, just west of Steens Mountain, where they established P Ranch. Moving boldly and aggressively, French bought up homesteads, used dummy entrymen to fraudulently gain other homesteads, and captured much-needed water sources. By the 1880s French and Glenn ran thirty thousand cattle and three thousand horses on the 132,000 acres of the French-Glenn Livestock Company.

Other cattle barons soon arrived on the scene. Henry Miller and Charles Lux, butchering and livestock barons of California, came north in the 1880s. Competing with them, among others, were W. B. Todhunter and John Devine of Todhunter-Devine and David Shirk. These range kings carved up southeastern Oregon into cattle country fiefdoms by manipulating complex federal land laws, through shrewd and sometimes ruthless legal and illegal dealings, and often with abundant capital. Sometimes violent and often colorful, they dominated the region, but their tactics frequently led to conflicts, as they did in the 1890s.

These conflicts arose largely out of shifting economic pressures on the cattle kings, as well as the increasing influx of sheepmen and homesteaders into the Steens country. Lessened rainfall, tough winters in 1884–85 and 1890, and a national economic panic in 1893 and its aftermath hastened along changes and confrontations. Once the cattle tycoons felt the increasing pinch of these transformations they were less hospitable to tenders of woolies and incoming settlers. In the years surrounding 1900 new settlers were congregating around the town of Burns in the northern section of Harney County, increasingly challenging the dominion and power of the cattle kings ensconced in the southern reaches of the county. Even more divisive were the controversies over land rights, fencing, and limited water supplies. They added explosive fuel to already smoldering discontents.

The explosion came in 1897, the day after Christmas, when homesteader Ed Oliver murdered Pete French. It is, one authority contends, "the most controversial single incident" in the history of Harney County. The sensational event carries both historical and symbolic import. For nearly a decade French had been trying to hound homesteaders and squatters off the vast holdings of the French-Glenn empire. Taking citizens and interlopers to court and even physically attacking opponents with his fists, French increasingly represented what some contemporaries considered the bloated arrogance of the cattle kings. When a jury with homesteader-settler sympathies acquitted Oliver on the questionable grounds of self-defense, the decision suggested that the dominating power of the range barons might be crumbling. Symbolically, Oliver had toppled the county's most well-known citizen, "the most towering and imposing member of the community," a historian notes.

The three decades from the late 1890s to the closing of the 1920s illustrated the large changes underway in areas surrounding the Steens. Although a few cattle kings remained in power after French's demise, most began the gradual transition from large, open-range cattle raising to the more compact and structured form of stock farming, with new attention to fencing and the raising of hay. Another transition became clear in the livestock census of 1900. In that year Harney County listed seventy-one thousand head of cattle but one hundred thirty thousand sheep. (The tax rolls of the county, notoriously suspect in accuracy, recorded three or four times that many sheep.) The numbers were even more revealing in Malheur County to the east with eighty-one thousand cattle and two hundred ninety-five thousand sheep. Year by year fewer resident and transient sheepmen were trailing their bands eastward to mining markets; more and more were buying their own range or, as the transient sheep raisers did, finding out-of-the-way and unappropriated lands, including those on Steens Mountain, on which to summer their bands. The limited range "war" in the Steens region, much less heated than in many other areas of eastern Oregon and the intermountain West, was largely between resident landowners (including sheepmen) and the "tramp" sheepmen who pushed illegally onto public lands hoping for weeks and even months of free grazing for their homeless bands. By the 1920s government grazing regulations and enforcement of those laws had yet to catch up with the ongoing competition for grazing on public lands in Harney County. That would happen in the next decade.

Meanwhile increasing numbers of homesteaders and other settlers were moving into Harney County. New and enlarged homestead acts, adding expanded provisions to the original Homestead Act of 1862, encouraged new settlers to immigrate to eastern Oregon. So did the wet years of abundant rainfall in the early twentieth century. Boosterism on the part of regional newspapers, land developers, and other promoters also played large roles. Romantic notions about owning one's own land, living independently in the wide-open West, and making thousands of dollars overnight likewise stirred the emotions of possible migrants. One deceiving come-on read: "[T]here are pastures there [the Pacific Northwest] that turn out 250 pound sheep and 2,200 pound cattle. There is no winter cold, no summer heat, no blizzards, no drought, and no crop failures." Believing such blarney, the homesteaders came quickly, like a trout chasing a new lure. Indeed, the years between 1907 and 1918, the "homesteaders' era," saw hundreds of newcomers taking up the "last dry hillocks" of Harney County. Population in the county jumped from 2,598 in 1900 to 4,059 in 1910, but the bust had already set in by 1920 with population dropping 1.7 percent to 3,992.

Concurrently, Burns, the only town of any size in the county, expanded from 719 in 1900, to 904 in 1910, and 1,022 in 1920.

The homestead era imploded as precipitously as it had boomed. With the return of dry years ("the dry cycle") and the collapse of transportation and irrigation schemes, newcomers, failing to overcome these and other climactic and economic challenges, could not "prove up" on their homesteads and left eastern Oregon. In 1930, the very year that the O'Keeffes took up their homestead near Fields, the distinguished American geographer Isaiah Bowman found only nineteen of seventy "houses and shanties" occupied along the lonesome road from Bend to Burns. One unsuccessful and disillusioned settler told Bowman, "I wouldn't give a nickel for a whole section of it." Across central and eastern Oregon, from the Fort Rock and Christmas Lake areas on the west, through the areas south of Burns, to other sections of Harney County on the east, homesteaders by the hundreds who had come with high hopes were abandoning their dreams of becoming successful landowners on the "last homestead frontier in America."

By the 1920s it had become manifestly clear that a homesteader taking up land in southeastern Oregon had less-than-best lands available for selection. The remaining marginal lands were often too arid for crop farming, and sometimes, in dry weather, contained insufficient pasturage for grazing animals. Besides aridity and drought, distance from needed transportation grids and markets remained vexing challenges. Failed ventures resulting from these experiences frequently led to rueful hindsights. One eastern Oregonian in Baker County, remembering his family's experiences, recalled that they "spent 11 years trying to prove you could grow grain with 10 inches of rainfall average yearly on soil suitable for grazing livestock, jack rabbits, and antelope."

The interwar decades were especially difficult times for agriculturists. In the years immediately following World War I, prices plummeted after wartime highs because of shrinking domestic and global demands and also because of mounting economic and diplomatic uncertainties. As a result, hard times zapped farmers and livestock ranchers well before the Great Depression fell like a huge wet blanket on all Americans in

1929. Adding to homesteaders' dilemmas was the fact that many of them had never been on farms or ranches of any kind. Instead, they had been lured from their clerical, urban, and often unexciting positions by romantic dreams of opportunity and a "main chance," lured into a taxing occupation for which they were inexperienced and ill prepared. As one disgruntled observer put it, with a bit of hyperbole, the lot of homesteaders was like that of a murderer: "servitude for life at hard labor without recompense—but without a murderer's guarantee of enough to eat."

Not every avenue was cut off and closed out for ambitious homesteaders in the early twentieth century, however. One historian notes an anomaly:

> One exception remained. Only on Steens Mountain was there still a good deal of unclaimed or unregulated public property and a near bonanza of both minerals and grass. In consequence the mountain produced the nearest thing to a state of nature in southeastern Oregon—an intermingling of Basque and Irish sheepherders scouring for free range, rawboned cowboys herding cattle from the P Ranch, homesteaders hugging isolated segments of the mountain slope.

It was to this exceptional place that the O'Keeffe family came, and they avoided most of the pitfalls of the 1930s and early 1940s because their goals were more modest—and realistic. They would graze sheep in an area that could sustain a limited number of livestock. They would not attempt to cultivate soil too arid and infertile to raise crops. And they would do nearly all of their own work. By careful, tight-budget planning and frugal living Benjamin and Izola O'Keeffe and their family hung on and succeeded for more than a decade while many others failed and fled their homesteads. All around nearby Bend and Burns, especially in areas south of these two towns, stood abandoned and boarded-up shanties of homesteaders who had failed and fled.

The Taylor Grazing Act (1934) represented another challenge facing the O'Keeffes and homesteaders raising livestock: the central government was beginning to regulate how grazing animals were to use federal lands. The Taylor Act, though beneficial for pasturelands and ranchers in the long run, nonetheless wrought controversial changes for grazers in the mid-to-late 1930s. Most livestock raisers looked on the legislation as cattlemen might have reacted to an all-mutton menu at a barbecue. The act, as part of President Franklin D. Roosevelt's far-reaching New Deal, sought to bring order out of rangeland chaos. Rather than allowing cattle and sheep raisers pell-mell entry into and indiscriminant use of federal grazing and forestlands, the government was attempting to protect fragile landscapes from overgrazing and to allot grazing lands on an equitable basis. But for many livestock raisers who had done as they pleased for several decades this enactment of 1934 was as unpopular as anything the government implemented in the 1930s, save the even more controversial federal decision to reduce livestock holdings to try to bring supply and demand into better balance. The Taylor Grazing Act was benchmark legislation. Since then, the federal government has increasingly protected its federal lands from overgrazing and attempted, through several means, to limit the number of animals allowed onto these fragile lands. Not many homesteaders, cattlemen, or sheepmen supported these path-breaking moves in the mid-1930s.

In their willingness to stay put despite all the difficulties they faced in the 1930s, the O'Keeffe family epitomized what noted western author Wallace Stegner defined as "stickers." They held on and stayed even though the Great Depression broadsided their nation, state, and county during the decade. When tight times forced the bank to take the family's sheep, they began again. So difficult were these years in Harney County that nearly 10 percent of its residents left. The county's population dropped from 5,920 in 1930 to 5,374 in 1940. Burns, hosting about half of the county's inhabitants, also lost population (from 2,599 to 2,566) during the depression decade. Pluck and determination kept the O'Keeffes on their homestead. In addition to their 160-acre homestead acreage, they utilized grazing rights to nearby lands and also secured another homestead twenty-fives miles away on top of the Steens for summer pasture.

But in the early 1940s a different kind of challenge finally drew them away. In the fall of 1942 Eileen turned fifteen, ready for high school. But there was none close by to Fields, so after boarding part of the family for a time in Burns, all the O'Keeffes moved there permanently for the education of their older daughter, and then her younger brother Johnny and sister Kathleen. Education was important for the O'Keeffes. They had earlier wintered some years in Fields so that their children could attend school. Izola helped in the school, and Benjamin was a devoted reader and poet, and superb storyteller. The move to Burns was not surprising since they had family and friends there, and it served as their shopping site. So after a dozen years on the demanding, unyielding homestead, the O'Keeffes moved to town, to demonstrate once again the ambition and perseverance so often displayed in their home at the base of Steens Mountain.

Some four to five hundred miles straight north in eastern Washington, in equally out-of-the-way rangelands, the Etulain family experienced similar challenges, if on a different scale. My Basque immigrant father, my mother of sod-house frontier heritage, and their three sons also faced isolation, demanding weather, and other foes crouched at our ranch doors. We also matched wits with coyotes, badgers, and roving, vicious dogs gone wild. These challenges bred a taciturnity, dedication to hard work, and frugality that my parents tried to pass on to their rascally sons. Mom evangelized for education, social propriety, and polish, and Dad preached dependability and fortitude (what the Basques called *indarra*) and long days of labor. He never gave up on his favorite sermons, often trying later to sneak a favorite bumper sticker on his three sons' cars: "Eat more lamb; 10,000 coyotes can't be wrong."

Other parallels with and differences from the O'Keeffes marked our sheep story in eastern Washington. We also confronted challenges of distance and what to do about schooling. After four years at a one-room school, which was five miles from our ranch and enrolled only five students, we three boys were forced into a one-hour trip twice a day to attend schools in the small town of Ritzville when my older brother started high school. Our classmates at the town school, largely the sons and daughters of German and Russian wheat farmers, knew the Etulain boys lied when we told them our sheep ranch sprawled out over ten thousand acres. Anything more than a section of ground seemed impossible to them. Of course we never admitted that rocks might be our most successful crop.

Means of transportation and available markets were other challenges. Spokane, nearly seventy miles away, was the closest market and only for a few lambs and calves. Because the Pacific Northwest had not yet developed a large appetite for lamb (the region lacked a sizeable population of Jewish and Mediterranean-heritage peoples), Dad was compelled to take his annual crop of five to ten thousand lambs, wethers, and old ewes to the Twin Cities or Chicago, thousands of miles to the east over the old Milwaukee Railroad. The Depression also put the squeeze on the Etulain family, but World War II changed everything. Huge new markets for wool, lamb, and mutton turned the corner for us. The tight times were in the past. Before long we too moved to town and became city kids.

And then there were those final differences. We had only saintly Basque herders, of course; none in need of premature burying as in Eileen's memoir. But those wild Irishmen, they were another story.

Ethnic chuckles aside, twenty-first century readers will recognize the spirit and perseverance necessary to homestead and ranch and to survive in these isolated backcountries of the Pacific Northwest. The O'Keeffe family challenged the stark, demanding landscape of the Steens Mountain foothills and wrestled out a spare but impressive life from that scene. The grit and grace of Eileen O'Keeffe McVicker's life (told through her able writerly helpmate Barbara Scot) provides a satisfying and fulfilling coming-of-age story that emboldens our courage even as it warms our hearts.

Suggested Readings

Bishop, Ellen Morris. *In Search of Ancient Oregon: A Geological and Natural History*. Portland, OR: Timber Press, 2003.

Bowman, Isaiah. *The Pioneer Fringe*. New York: American Geographical Society, 1931.

Etulain, Richard W. *Beyond the Missouri: The Story of the American West*. Albuquerque: University of New Mexico Press, 2006.

Jackman, E. R., and R. A. Long. *The Oregon Desert*. Caldwell, ID: Caxton Printers, 1965.

Jackman, E. R., John Scharff, and Charles Conkling. *Steens Mountain in Oregon's High Desert Country*. Caldwell, ID: Caxton Printers, 1967.

Lamar, Howard R., ed. *The New Encyclopedia of the American West*. New Haven, CT: Yale University Press, 1998.

Loy, William G., ed., et al. *Atlas of Oregon*. 2d ed. Eugene: University of Oregon Press, 2001.

Pomeroy, Earl. *The American Far West in the Twentieth Century*. New Haven, CT: Yale University Press, 2008.

Pratt, Alice Day. *A Homesteader's Portfolio*. New York: Macmillan Co., 1922. Reprinted by Oregon State University Press, Corvallis, with an introduction by Molly Gloss, 1993.

Robbins, William G. *Landscapes of Promise: The Oregon Story 1800-1940*. Seattle: University of Washington Press, 1997.

Simpson, Peter K. *The Community of Cattlemen: A Social History of the Cattle Industry in Southeastern Oregon, 1869-1912*. Moscow: University of Idaho Press, 1987.

Part I

Steens Mountain

I WAS AN OUTDOOR CHILD ALL MY LIFE. Our home was in a very remote area: high rugged sagebrush and juniper tree country. We lived at the southern end of Steens Mountain and had a wonderful view of the Pueblo Mountain range. The big mountain had snow on the top all year round in those days and the air made it look blue. In the morning we children would wake early and walk a mile or two up high just to see down in the valley.

There would be deer feeding quietly in the rim of big rocks; lichen in many colors, which we could see if we looked closely; stones to gather for our pockets; and wildflowers that grew in abundance in the shade of the rimrock where it was cool and moist. My mother knew the names of many of the flowers but when we found a new variety, we named it ourselves. We gathered the flowers in armfuls and when we took them to our mother, she filled the galvanized washtub with water for us to put them in. This was during the Great Depression when nobody had any money.

WITH A MOTHER WHO HAD banished the word can't from our language and a father who recited poetry while herding his sheep, we didn't dare dwell on the negative. For one thing, we just didn't have time. My dad could walk faster than a horse, a well-known fact on Steens Mountain, and my mom firmly believed that you could do anything you set your mind to if you just got busy and did it. Not every day, however, of that time that people call the good old days was good. Certainly not a day when you'd had a run-in with a rabid coyote.

✦

WE DIDN'T HAVE MODERN CONVENIENCES like running water at the homestead. My dad's plan to siphon off a stream from a spring just up the hill came to naught when the flow turned out to be seasonal. I'm not exactly sure when that fact became apparent, but the folks were so in love with the view from the site they had chosen for the house that they wouldn't have changed the location anyway, certainly not for a minor inconvenience like carrying water.

A more reliable, year-round spring came out of the mountain about a quarter of a mile from the house. That meant we carried our buckets up and down the hills and around the draws in a regular bucket brigade. We used pails that the lard came in and old cream cans that fit in a little wooden wagon Dad made my brother for Christmas one year. He painted it pale green as that was the only color paint that was available. Mom or Dad would pull the little wagon; sometimes they had to have a push from behind. I always carried two of the buckets. This was our entire water supply until we ran out and it was time to go again.

We made that trip almost every day and for the most part, it was an uneventful stroll or a family chore we did together, so it didn't seem a chore at all. And it certainly never occurred to us that it was a hardship. No one we knew had running water, not in the little town of Fields, nor did our cousins near Burns who had wells that were closer to their houses. But Dad always came right back from the spring when he went alone so we should have known right away that something was wrong when he took so long. Mom was inside cooking dinner and my little brother Johnny and I were feeding the bummer lambs.

Bummer lambs are lambs that have lost their mothers, or maybe the mother had twins that year and not enough milk to feed them both. We were using a nanny goat that Dad had borrowed because she had so much milk and we had so many lambs. She would let her own kid suck but she didn't like sharing her milk with the lambs. Johnny had to hold her by the chin whiskers so she wouldn't bite the lambs while I held the lambs in place to suck. We had just come in from our chores when Mom asked us if we had seen Dad anywhere as she had dinner ready.

She sent us back outside to look for him, but he wasn't on the path. Suddenly we heard him hollering, and there he was way up on the side of the hill where he had gone to get rocks to throw because he didn't have any other weapon with him. "Get the gun, get the gun!" he was yelling. He still carried the galvanized buckets of water.

Johnny and I knew that this was a bad situation. We started hollering for Mom and she came running out of the house to see what was wrong. At first we didn't see the coyote but then it came into view from behind a big bush of sagebrush, awfully close behind Dad. It was weaving from side to side and its head was swaying. Mom knew at once what was happening because she had seen rabid animals before this one. "You kids get inside and stay there," she said, so we ran into the house and watched from the window. Then Mom tore out with the rifle.

Now Mom could shoot a gun, but she was a long way from the coyote, and maybe she didn't know how many bullets she had or maybe she was afraid she'd miss the coyote—I don't know. This was a shot that had to be straight and true. Johnny went back out on the porch so he could see more and Mom yelled at me to make him go back in the house, so I did. We'd all heard tales of men who had been bitten by rabid animals. There was no sure cure for rabies then, and even if there had been, the closest hospital to give the series of painful shots was in Winnemucca, Nevada. Without treatment the person would die a horrible death and in the meantime would be dangerous to others. Later I heard a terrible story of people in Oklahoma and Texas that had rabies and were tied to trees until they died. My little sister stood on the sofa and watched from the window.

Dad set down the pails of water and Mom stopped in the path. You could see they were figuring out what to do but they had to figure it out fast. The coyote swayed closer and when it realized that Dad had stopped, it lunged forward. That's when Dad threw a rock that glanced off the coyote's shoulder and bounced down the hill. The coyote was close enough now that even we kids could see the white at its mouth and the frantic, bewildered shake of its head. Momentarily it was completely confused by the rock, and then it whirled and chased it down the hill, biting and biting in its uneven run.

Mom and Dad ran toward each other and Dad grabbed for the gun. We kids were all pressed against the window and none of us said a single word. When the sick animal turned again to find him, Dad shot it between the eyes and it dropped right down on the ground as if grateful to stop. Mom grabbed at Dad, then, and we could see that she was shaking.

After Dad was sure the coyote was dead, they each picked up a pail of water, which had not even spilled, and started back toward the house. After dinner we all went to look at the dead coyote. A rabid coyote has a black tongue, and this coyote had a black tongue, all right; we saw that when the folks dug a hole and buried it.

✢

ON MARCH 20, 1920, MY FATHER, Benjamin Joseph O'Keeffe, then twenty-three years old, left Ireland on *The Laplander* for the United States. It took him a month on the ship to get to Ellis Island; from there he boarded a train for Lakeview, Oregon. In Lakeview some Irishmen who had been in Oregon for some time met him. They whisked him off to the Lakeview Hotel, where they fed him and gave him lodging for the night. Early the next morning he was taken out to a sheep camp to herd sheep in Lake County, west of Silver Lake, Oregon.

There were a lot of Irish in Oregon then; the sheepherders were Irish, Scotch-Irish, or Basque. An Irishman named Singleton sponsored my dad, and later Dad sponsored others who came from Ireland. Some came to Oregon and stayed like my father and some, like his brothers who came later, went on to other places after they started out as sheepherders. Life with the sheep wasn't for everybody—one of my dad's brothers who came first to Oregon went to the California gold fields and another brother ended up in Chicago as a fireman for thirty-five years. But my father knew what he wanted. He loved the big country and he wanted to have his own ranch, to be a sheep man, not just a herder hired to watch the sheep. At first he worked for Mr. Singleton, taking ewe lambs instead of pay. After six years he had a nice band of his own, and he needed a place to run them. He headed for southeastern Oregon, where he found winter pasture on a ranch in the Catlow Valley. There he set up camp and watched over his sheep.

MY DAD WAS THE OLDEST of eight children; he had six brothers and one sister. He was born in Glendalougha, County Kerry, over by Kilarney, in 1897. He graduated from high school in Ireland, which, according to him, was about the equivalent of college in the United

States in those days. To get enough money for passage to the United States, he worked in the shipyards in Scotland. He could have been anything, because he was so smart, but he wanted to ranch and be with the sheep. He loved the sheep and so did I. As a very small child I would be out in the middle of the band of sheep, looking at each one and loving them. I had white hair and sometimes they couldn't find me among the sheep.

DAD ALWAYS HAD A NOTEBOOK with him and while watching the sheep, he would sit on a rock and write poetry. And he loved to tell stories. Sometimes the stories were Irish myths, like the one about the castles in the sky, or about strange apparitions he had seen. He had lived in an abandoned castle in Ireland called The Lindfield House when he was a teenager, working for a castle caretaker. His job was to take visitors for a tour of the castle and to give its history.

My dad told story after story about this castle and later as an adult I went to see it—it is still standing. The English burned it in one of their wars but it is identifiable in its ruined state. Some of the gargoyles remain and a little of the fancy trimming around the top of the ceiling tells you that this castle once was quite elaborate. Dad talked about the big barn on the ground level where the cows had been kept and the ramp where the horses went to the upper level. I was able to find those places, although I didn't see the ghostly lantern of my favorite Irish story.

That story got mixed in with other mysterious experiences with apparitions. These "ghosts" went up and down the stairway where Dad and the caretaker slept and Dad said he could walk right through them without feeling a thing except a breath of cold air. He heard chains clanking too. The part I liked best, though, was about the lantern. Every night it was my dad's job to milk the cow that was kept at the castle for the caretaker. So he would go down to the lower level where the cow was kept, the same place where the cattle had been kept in the old days when the castle was still in use. He milked the cow by hand, of course, because that's the way it was done then, just the way it was still done when I learned as a child, and he sat on a little stool.

Just as he was settling in to milk, with his forehead against the soft side of the cow, the light would appear off to one side. It was a strange glow exactly at the height a man would carry a lantern. It wasn't a scary kind of light; in fact, it was rather dark in the lower level of the castle so it seemed a friendly thing that this lantern-level glow would accompany him all the while he was tending to the cow and milking her. When he was all done for the night, the light would disappear into the big wooden doors at the back of the castle.

Dad was interested in science and he was not at all superstitious. And he liked most everybody he met, so I guess he felt friendly toward the ghosts too. Strange things didn't scare him; in fact, he was quite practical about them. He thought if he stayed around he could figure them out in time and develop a theory for them just like he did for the castles in the sky that people talked about. There were all sorts of stories of exact replicas of castles that people had seen in the sky right down to the very details of the architecture. Dad had actually seen the castles in the sky himself, but he didn't think they were so much magic as they were an odd physical phenomena involving phosphorous. His theory, which for a child listening was as mysterious as the myth, was that the phosphorous created a mirror image of the castle that was projected in the sky against clouds under certain conditions.

LATER HIS FAMILY MOVED SOUTH of Limerick, and one of the castles near where they lived at that time was Old Palace Ghriene. That was a hard time for Irish families that had grown close in the winters with their long nights of stories. One by one the older brothers left for America, some to Oregon and some to other places. Dad wrote home faithfully to his mother, but some of the brothers were never heard from again, like the two who went to Alaska. Later we found out that one had drowned when he fell off a log into a river and another died with his dog tied to him while he was lost in a blizzard. The men who found him after the snow had stopped had to fight off the dog, which had started to eat his leg.

IN THE WINTER MY DAD WOULD TELL stories that would go on from one dark night to the next. Later I told lots of stories myself, especially when we visited our cousins in Burns and we were all piled on the bed crosswise like cordwood, the girls on one end and the younger boys on the bottom. I could make the stories go from one night to the next too, but Dad was the greatest storyteller. We all loved listening to him and I don't remember thinking the nights were long, even though there was no electricity in the valleys by Steens Mountain in those days. Our lights were coal-oil lamps, and every day or so, the lamps had to be filled. We spent a lot of time in the dark.

MY MOTHER'S FAMILY WAS A MIXTURE of German and Scotch-Irish, and her parents met in Missouri where they were already second-generation Americans, raised in the States. My grandfather, Charles Benjamin Ausmus, migrated west during the gold rush and never got any farther than southeastern Oregon. My grandmother, Lillian Ludella Standley, whom he had married in Missouri, came west on the train as far as Ontario, Oregon, and from there she and their two small boys came by freight wagon to Burns. They homesteaded and raised cattle and horses. That is where my mother was born on August 18, 1905, a girl in a family of four boys. When she was nine years old, her oldest brothers had a sheep-shearing business, and they hired my mom to cook for the shearing and haying crews. She had to do all the baking of bread, pies, and cakes too.

The oldest brother went to World War I, and while he was there, my mother and her brother Standley went to high school. They stayed in the oldest brother's cabin all week and at night they knitted socks to sell for the soldiers. On weekends they came home to the family ranch and rounded up the wild cows from the herd. After they got them in a corral, they tied them up and milked them. My grandmother put the milk in shallow pans so the cream could rise better and when Mom and her brother went back to school they took the milk cans to town. They sold the milk for money to live on while they were in school. After high school Standley went east to Chicago Coin Electrical School and Mom went to normal school in Monmouth, Oregon, for one year. Her first teaching job was in the Catlow Valley, near the little town of Blitzen, which had a store and a post office.

THIS PRETTY BLOND TEACHER boarded with the rancher where my father wintered his sheep. Every morning and evening she had to walk across my father's pasture through the sheep to get to work, and pretty soon that Irish sheepherder had followed her to the school. He got the children to laugh by making faces through the window, and she didn't know what was going on and scolded the children. But soon she figured out what he was doing and got even with him. While he was busy making faces through the window she sneaked up behind him with a pail of water and threw it over his head. The kids loved it.

ON JANUARY 29, 1927, Nancy Izola Ausmus and Benjamin Joseph O'Keeffe were married. That spring they lived out in the sheep camp with the sheep on the range, with all nature beckoning at their tent door: the wildlife, the flowers, the shrubs and trees, and with the companionship of each other and their horses to ride. For the winter they leased a ranch in the Trout Creek area with a beautiful old house and lots of pasture for the sheep. A baby girl was born at the end of November. That was me.

✦

I HAVE NEVER BEEN BORED in my life. When I was two-and-a-half years old, my folks moved from the leased ranch at Trout Creek to a homestead claim five miles north of the town of Fields, Oregon. This was on the southern foothills of Steens Mountain, in the part of Oregon called the Great Basin or High Desert country. Steens Mountain is truly unique among mountains; it rises over 9,700 feet out of a flat landscape with the Alvord Desert on the eastern side. To the west and north toward the town of Burns, it is flat too, although not quite the desert that it is to the east. There are large shallow remnants of the giant lakes that once covered the entire area. Glaciers carved out fantastic canyons and gorges on the Steens, but they couldn't flatten it out.

OUR HOUSE ON THE SOUTHERN SLOPE of Steens Mountain was built by my father and his brother with the help of other Irish herders. They started in the fall of the year and we lived in tents while they were working on it. While I have little memory of this time, my mother once started to write down the details of the building of it and left this account:

"SEVERAL OF THE IRISH BOYS who owned sheep and lived in the desert came to help build the house. It took longer than anticipated due to the long hauls over the bad roads to bring in lumber. Fall was creeping up on us and before long snow, lots of it. The house was progressing and by Christmas the petitions were in and rooms partly floored and a small portion of the house was roofed. The temperature went to forty below zero and we moved from the tents into the one room, which had a roof for our beds and the kitchen. I kept a roaring fire with the coffee and teapots full and lots of food ready on the stove, even homemade bread and rolls. All were happy and the work went on. Care had to be taken not to touch the nails with bare hands as the steel would stick and freeze to the skin. Once while working on the roof, Ben forgot and put some nails in his mouth. Needless to say he had a sore mouth for some time after that.

Our baby girl Eileen was over two-and-a-half years old now, and she had to see all that was going on, so we let her go back and forth to the tent camp thirty yards below the house. We had to keep a close eye on her as the snow was now two feet deep. The men waded through it and the trails immediately drifted full but most of the places the snow was crusted enough that Eileen could walk on top of the snow. Sometimes she broke through and dropped in until only her face or the top of her head was above snow level. On these occasions a loud howl went up and a rescue was made. None of this dampened her spirits, and she continued her trips to and from the camp about thirty yards from the house. No one had colds that winter and a hardier baby never lived."

BY THE NEXT WINTER THE HOUSE was a tight, enclosed shell with a ceiling in the living room and one of the front windows already in. It had also become a regular stop for the Irish and Basque herders who brought their bands of sheep past our place on the way down the mountain to the valleys for hay. Later, when my dad put up a tin barn, he let herders store some of their extra gear there when they went up the mountain for the summer. They put their horses in our corral if they stayed for the night, which they nearly always did. The year they were still building the house was one of early and unexpected heavy snow, and my mother's account details the hardships the herders who were trapped higher on the mountain with their bands of sheep encountered.

"OUR PLACE, ONLY THREE-QUARTERS of a mile from the top of the southern Steens Mountain pass, became a haven for many who might otherwise have frozen to death. From one who collapsed at the doorway to six or seven at a time who had been stranded in the pass known as Long Hollow. This winter as many as eleven thousand sheep were brought through Long Hollow over the summit and down to our place for the night. The snow was so deep that trails had to be broken and the bands brought through one at a time. When one band had reached the valley below and those sheep were out of the deep snow, everyone went back to break more trail and bring through another band. This continued until all the sheep were through.

Some of the men stayed with the sheep, and the rest made their headquarters at our house, working from there to try to save the animals that were marooned in the deep snow. We had only one extra bedroom. Three men shared a bedspread on the living room floor, one slept on the daveno, and five shared one bed in the bedroom. The men slept crosswise on the bed.

The men had cut strips of gunnysacks and wrapped their legs over the top of their pants up to their knees to keep the snow from freezing their legs. These could not be taken off until they thawed for a while, so the men sat around the room and great puddles of water melted from their legs and ran across my floors, which were linoleum and could be wiped up easily. Little Eileen busied herself the best she knew how to help her mother. She went to the back storage room and brought out dry gunnysacks and told the men they had best put their feet on the sacks and not let the water run around on Mama's clean floors. She afforded the young Irish boys who had no families a good deal of amusement and needless to say was quite a favorite."

THIS IS THE HOUSE WHERE I SPENT my childhood with the rest of my family: my father and mother, my younger brother and sister, and much of the time, my grandmother as well. Six of us in that little house that was twenty-four foot square. During those years I didn't

think it was small inside; maybe it was because we lived in such big country and spent most of our time outside.

I GREW UP WITH THE ANIMALS, most of all with the sheep, as my dad's band numbered over two thousand at its highest count, but also with dogs, horses, a milk cow (or, if the cow wasn't fresh, a nanny goat), and the big black mule. Then all the wild animals, some not invited, like the coyotes and rattlesnakes. It was a hard, happy life with layers of riches.

✢

I WAS TAUGHT NEVER TO WASTE TIME. My grandmother (my mother's mother) lived with us off and on and she taught me to sew by hand and to do embroidery. I had a little wicker rocking chair, which was usually kept beside Grandma's big wicker rocker, and she and I would sit and sew together. There were always socks to darn and mending to do. Not only did I do my own, I also did the darning and mending for the rest of them, my parents and my younger brother and sister. After I got older, I helped sew clothes for all of us. Time is valuable, said both my mother and grandmother, and there is so much to learn in life that there isn't time for it all. Even now, when my mother has been gone a long time, I think of her teaching me that when I sit down to rest.

MY GRANDMA SPENT MUCH OF HER TIME working in the garden while Mom cared for the rest of the family, helped Dad with the outside work, and did the cooking. That garden provided much of our food for the year, and even when we went to the higher pastures on the Steens with the sheep, Grandma stayed to tend it. We all helped when we were there. First Dad would plow the ground with the team of horses and a hand plow. It was a family affair to plant all the seeds and potatoes. We children loved the big plowed area to play in and the smell of the fresh dirt.

As a little girl I spent hours and hours with my grandmother. She and I would go into the garden early in the morning before anyone else was awake and watch the sun come up. It was a beautiful time with the crisp blue sky and the sun like a giant fireball coming over the mountains. In the spring she and I would race to see who would find the first wild buttercups on the hill above our house. I loved to go hunting through the brush early in the morning with the smell of the ground steaming from the sun's warm rays. There it would be, the first little yellow flower, peeking out from under a rock or a sagebrush bush. Under the rimrock the flowers were bigger and thicker than in other places because it was a protected area with more moisture. After the buttercups came the wild pansies, the birdbills, and the yellow Johnny-jump-ups. We celebrated them all.

When we went to the garden, we would often stay all day. We grew potatoes and tomatoes and just about everything else. Everything was planted from seed, some in the house, kept by the window to get an early start. You have never tasted a good ear of corn until you have eaten one under a sunflower in the garden along with some raw carrots and cucumbers. I especially loved the cantaloupe and the watermelons. There was a spring above the garden that my dad dug out, with a team of horses and a shovel-like piece of machinery we called a Fresno, to make a pond with a little dirt dam to irrigate. This was not good water for drinking, but it was good for the garden. Hoses with pieces of screen wire tied to the end to keep them from clogging were put into the water and primed with water poured in one end. Water flowed by gravity through the hoses, over the little dirt dam and into the garden where Grandma would guide it into shallow ditches she made with her hoe.

This provided a bountiful harvest. Mom and Grandma did a lot of canning in the late summer. They also made rhubarb jam, tomato jam, watermelon preserves, and sometimes, wild chokecherry jam. Grandma also grew some raspberries and strawberries, but we usually ate them fresh. There weren't any freezers or refrigerators, so if we wanted to keep things cool for daily use in the summer, we had a frame like a cupboard on legs that my folks had made. The frame was covered with flour sacks that were wet and had been dipped in starch. These sacks would stretch when pulled and they were nailed to the frame. The starch would make them tighter and keep them from letting in as much dust. These frames were put on the shady side of the house with a dishpan of water on the top. Clean gunnysacks were necessary to complete this refrigeration technique. The end of one sack was placed in the pan of water and held down with a rock while the rest of the sacks were placed to hang down the sides of the cupboard. The first sack acted like a wick to draw the water through the other sacks. As the breeze blew, the evaporation resulted in a cool pantry for milk and butter. We could make Jell-O at night and it would set by morning, but if it was very warm, we had to eat it early in the day before it melted.

The root vegetables would go in the cellar in the fall. There was a bin in the back to fill with sand, which we did by putting a galvanized washtub in the trunk of the car. We would fill the tub with load after load of clean sand at a dry creek bed. At the harvest in went the turnips, parsnips, carrots, potatoes, and even the heads of cabbage. They would last through the winter there. The first root cellar was made in a hurry and it was a hole dug down about four or five feet deep with a roof made of willow boughs, gunnysacks, and dirt. Dad carried the willows from the stand by the creek in a bundle on his back. Eggs were stored in a crock and it was my job to go to the cellar and get the eggs, I suppose because I was the oldest and I was not so apt to drop the bowl.

I hated getting the eggs. It had to do with darkness and snakes. In fact, I was scared to go in the cellar, but someone had to do it. As the oldest child I had a lot of chores to do, and I may have complained about the eggs, but I wouldn't have said much. Mom was pretty handy with the razor strap or the willow switch and my brother and I got it good if we forgot our chores or did something nasty to each other, like the time I hit Johnny with a coffee can. I felt awfully bad about hurting him, and Mom made sure I felt some of the pain too. Johnny and I thought my little sister Kathleen got off easy, but she must have gotten it too, because once she actually hid the strap. Until Mom found it, Dad had to use a piece of glass to sharpen his razor. You did what you were told when you were a kid, and you just didn't argue. I never once talked back to my folks, well, not until I was in high school. We all had our own chores, and we did them whether we wanted to or not.

It was total darkness in the root cellar when the door was closed, and it smelled of cool dirt. We had a broomstick that we kept outside. When we went in, we would grab the stick, open the door wide, and run the stick around the inside of the door and ceiling before we entered. The idea was to make a noise and alert snakes so they wouldn't attack you out of fear. I always stood there blinking into the darkness, imagining a snake hanging from the ceiling, but I never saw one that way. I suppose the bigger fear should have been stepping on one coiled on the floor. You found them that way sometimes by the sagebrush, all wound up and ready to strike. That's when they could get you; they could strike as far as their body length, so you needed to jump way back so as not to get hit.

So I'd stand there by the cellar door thinking about snakes, and then I had to walk across the little dark room to the big crock where we kept the eggs. It was filled with a salty brine to keep the eggs fresh, thick brine almost like a jelly that was cold and slimy like a snake belly, and I had to stick my hand down in it, sometimes way down if there weren't many eggs. It gives me snake shivers just to think about it. It was a trick to hold a slippery egg in your hand and transfer it to the bowl without dropping it and another trick not to drop the bowl after you got the eggs in it when your whole arm was slimy. And sure enough, there really were snakes in that ceiling.

ONE FALL WHEN THE MARKING CREW was there, I had just been sent down in the cellar to get some eggs for a cake. Marking crews castrated the male lambs and docked all the tails, so you needed several men to get the job done in a hurry. When Mom had a crew to cook for, she almost always made a cake, and she'd set up a wash station for the men right outside the root cellar door so they could clean up a bit before the meal. Ours was such a small house that things like washing up were often done outside. Mom would put a bucket of water out there, set the enamel basin on a bench with a bar of soap, and then she'd hang a towel on a stick. One year a man named Jerry Murphy was on the marking crew.

Jerry was a real wild Irishman and he always had us laughing with his bushy eyebrows that moved when he talked and his thick red hair that stuck straight up. When he gave a laugh, it wasn't a regular laugh at all but a snort, a loud monosyllabic *ha* that would sound like a clap of thunder. That day when he was washing up and had his face all lathered with soap, he reached for the towel. Right then this huge rattlesnake slipped out of the roof of the root cellar and slithered between his legs. Jerry saw it through all the soap, and "Ha!" he thundered, but he didn't mean it as a laugh. His eyebrows shot right up into his hair, which had stood up a couple of extra inches when he saw that rattler. He took off like the wild Irishman he was and he went running past the house and down the hill bellowing, "Snake!"

Everyone came tearing out of the house, sure that Jerry had been bitten. The last thing he should have done was run, but he was one scared Irishman! They cornered the snake and killed it and got Jerry back in the house, only to find he hadn't been bitten at all. But it made it even worse for me to go down in the cellar after the eggs. Where there was one snake, there could surely be another.

Not too long after that, my dad made a new cellar with rocks. We hauled stones from the hill beside the house in a wooden wheelbarrow that Dad made, and he put on a good wooden roof, which he covered with a layer of tar paper and a better door. Although it still had a floor of dirt, the floor was always swept and kept tidy. This new improved cellar was a nice one, with sturdy shelves for the canned goods and good wooden bins, just like people had in town.

IT WAS HARD TO KEEP ANY KIND of fresh meat, so we usually didn't have much meat in the summer except for bacon that the folks bought at the store in Fields. But in the fall Dad might get a deer once in a while. If the days were still warm, Mom would make jerky from the meat. First she would soak it in a salt and pepper brine, and after it had soaked for a few days, she hung it on the clothesline in strips. We kids would grab off hunks as we ran by, and if it was soft and rubbery it wasn't done, but if it cracked off it was ready.

To keep the meat that wasn't made into jerky fresh, Dad would wrap it in flour sacks, which he put into a wool sack during the day. If there was any hay in the barn, Dad would wrap it around the meat completely before we buried it. We dug holes as far under the shade of a big sage bush as possible and, before we put the meat in, lined them with grass to keep them clean and cool. Then we put kettles with tight lids into the holes, covered them with gunnysacks, and shoveled some dirt on top. At night Dad took the meat out of the hole and hung it from a long pole to keep it safe from hungry animals. Some people canned meat, but my folks didn't do much of that. There had been an epidemic of ptomaine poisoning, and they were rather scared of that happening to us.

Dad had ptomaine poisoning once when he was still just a herder and he was dependent on the camp tender to bring supplies. That was the way it was done for the big outfits that sent their herders out in the mountains with different bands of sheep. The herders weren't supposed to be left totally alone more than three days, but this tender went to town with the pack outfit and didn't come back for ten days. He had gone to town, gotten drunk, and passed out. That left Dad without any food. He said he picked up some of the old bread he had put out for the dogs and ate that. Then he was down to one can of tomatoes. He opened them and ate some, but he left some for the next day. He didn't want them to spoil so he dug a hole and put the can in a kettle and buried it. He was getting weak from hunger and his dogs were starving, too. The next night when the tender still didn't come back he dug up the tomatoes and ate them but he became deathly sick. He passed out on the floor of his tent. All told it was ten days before the tender returned with food, and Dad was just about dead, with the sheep scattered all over the hills. After that Dad wouldn't let the tender leave. He left him with the sheep and got the supplies himself.

WE NEVER ATE RABBITS, but lots of people did. The government infected the rabbits with a very fast-spreading disease that caused them to die. People caught it sometimes and some of them died, but some of them survived in the hospital in Winnemucca, Nevada; that I know.

SOMETIMES GRANDMA LEFT for a while to stay with my uncles near Burns. These uncles were my mom's brothers: Ormond, Standley, Dick, and Henry. I missed Grandma because she was a real friend for me, and she remained so all the rest of her life—we shared secrets, even when I was in high school, when we shared the biggest secret of all. We always went for walks, just Grandma and me, and I loved to go to the top of the hills. There was an outcropping of rimrock and one very big rock where Grandma used to lift me up to sit. Then she would say, "Now that makes a nice big seat for you, doesn't it?" I called it The Big Seat ever after and to this day, I can find it when I go back to hike in the hills. There was a bunch of wild mahogany on the north side, and we used to find lots of wildflowers there.

GRANDMA AND I SLEPT TOGETHER for a long time when she stayed with us. When the Irish sheepherders came to our house, they needed somewhere to sleep. One time one of the fellows said, "I am going to sleep in your bed."

I said, "No, you can't."

"Why?" he asked.

I said, "Because you can't." He kept at me and finally I said, "Well, I guess I could sleep on the floor and you could sleep with Grandma." That brought down the house.

✢

WOMEN HAD TO BE MIGHTY TOUGH in the foothills of Steens Mountain. When I was still a little girl, my dad nearly died one winter. He was so sick and his skin was so tender that he couldn't stand the weight of the covers on him. The snow was real deep that year, with drifts of ten feet in the canyons, and it was hard to keep the house warm. Our house was built of shiplap siding with no insulation and exposed rafters and ceiling joists. The folks did paper the living room, but the other rooms weren't papered. There was no money to complete it yet, and even if there had been money, it was hard to get materials there because they had to be hauled one hundred and thirty miles over rough dirt roads. Because Dad was sick, my mother had to get all the wood, and I remember standing on the davenport in front of the living room window, watching Mom pull sagebrush for a fire. She had a big pinto horse that she had been given as a wedding present by her brothers, and she would tie a long rope to her saddle horn. The pinto would pull until the brush came up, and she would drag the brush to the chopping block where she cut it into firewood.

Sagebrush burns fast so my mother had to do this for hours to keep the fire warm enough for my dad, who was so feverish that he could only keep the sheet on him. When the roads were passable, they finally got him to the hospital. The doctor said he would die or at least the illness would take away twenty years, but he pulled through and got strong again and worked hard the rest of his life. But that winter was terrible, and my mother worked awfully hard. We were over five miles from Fields, where she had to go for supplies. I had to be close to Dad so he could watch me while she rode down into the valley to the store. She had to go around snow drifts, so the trip could take more than two hours, and it was hard to keep the fire going that long. The winds were cold and the drifts were high.

WHEN YOU LIVED ON A RANCH, it was all hands on deck every morning. There was always more to do than could be done no matter how many people there were, and women worked just as hard as the men, maybe harder because they had the inside chores too. Mom hauled most of the water for the household and did the washing in a Maytag machine that had a gasoline motor. The water was heated outside over a bonfire in a galvanized tub before it was carried to the Maytag in buckets. When Dad was around he helped haul the water, but a lot of the time he was working or out with the sheep, so washing clothes was a process that took at least half a day. Mom ironed with an old flat iron that had to be heated on the woodstove. We thought we had it good when she got a new gas iron that burned white gas and was pumped up with a little hand pump.

MOM KEPT US ALL IN LINE, fed, bathed, and disciplined, and she lined out our chores every day. She sewed all our clothes until I got old enough to take over the job. A lot of mine were made over from the clothes the teacher from the school down in Fields gave me. This particular teacher dressed up very smart every day for school with heels and real expensive outfits. When she went home to visit her people in Salt Lake City in the summer, she'd give the year's wardrobe to my mother. Mom would rip the clothes apart at the seams, wash and iron the pieces, and then she would lay a pattern on however she could get it to fit. Mom made me real nice things, and when I outgrew them, she made them over again for my little sister Kathleen. When we would tear our clothes, she would make little butterflies from scraps to appliqué over the patched place and she would sew other butterflies around so you couldn't tell which one was the patch. She made shirts and pants for my brother too; she could sew absolutely everything. The house was always spotless, and when we kids went to school we started out clean and neat.

MY DAD LEARNED HOW TO COOK when he was a single sheepherder. He made delicious sourdough biscuits in a little homemade Dutch oven in the yard and fantastic pancakes in animal shapes that we kids loved. But Mom did most of the everyday cooking because Dad always had work to do outside. She had to make all our bread and pastry, and she made the best cinnamon rolls, which I can smell to this day. She cooked with sagebrush, which burns out real fast, so she was constantly filling the stove, trying to keep it at an even temperature so not to burn anything. Cow chips make a better and hotter fire, but we only had one cow in those days. Mom and Grandma did a lot of canning on that stove, preserving whatever they could for the winter. They made homemade butter too, patties the size of the crock, salted and layered until the crock was full. These crocks went down in the root cellar and were placed by the crock full of eggs.

HAVING BEEN RAISED ON A RANCH, Mom could buckaroo cows, ride horses, and do almost anything that needed to be done. She could throw hay bales on a wagon, pitch hay off the stack, and hitch the teams to machinery. She could change a tire, which might sound simple now, but there was a lot more to changing a tire back then. It meant jacking up the car and taking off the wheel, removing the tube, putting a patch on the hole, reinserting the tube in the tire, then filling the tire with the hand pump once she got it back on the car. She could even work on the motor if she had to.

We were always mashing the oil pan by high centering on rocks. Then she had to crawl under the car and take off the pan, pound out the dents with a rock, put it back on, and add new oil. I walked miles in front of the car in my childhood to guide Mom up and over and around the brush and big rocks, especially one summer when we were staying in the canyon on Wild Horse Creek north and west of Andrews and had to bring supplies to the family. I remember saying, "Mom, can't we just park and walk the rest of the way?" Mom would say, "I think we can get closer so we don't have to pack so much stuff to camp." My mom could take a car where most people wouldn't take a horse.

MOM USED TO TELL ME that there was no such word as *can't*. "You can do anything you want to do if you want to do it bad enough," she'd say, and it made no difference whether you were a woman or a man as to whether you could finish the job. She wore her jeans out to work and when she came in the house she would go to her bedroom and come out all fresh in a nice little cotton frock. By the time we had to go back outside after lunch she would be all dressed in her jeans and ready to go.

LITTLE KIDS WHO LIVED ON A RANCH had to be pretty tough too. During World War II when we were attending grade school five miles away in Fields, there was gas rationing. Mom would take us to school in the mornings after we had done our chores, but we had to walk home at night. It was downhill most of the way going to school but uphill all the way home on a mostly dirt road. We carried our books in our arms and studied all the way home so we would have our homework done. If one of us had a problem we talked about it, and by the time we got home we had probably figured it out. If not, it was up to Mom or Dad to help us.

We never thought of the walk as hard, though, as we picked up rocks and flowers and sticks to keep any bulls or rattlesnakes away. We got lots of exercise, and when we got home, there were those chores to do again—there were always chores to do on a ranch. We had to milk the nanny goat to feed the bummer lambs that had lost their mothers. Mom fed the lambs during the day, but in the morning and evening it was up to my brother and me to get it done.

SOMETIMES AFTER SCHOOL I had to walk up the mountains to see if any new lambs were born and to drive some of the sheep down to the corrals for the night. I used to have what they called growing pains, and my legs would feel like they were falling off, but in those days children didn't complain if they had aches and pains. Anyway, it didn't seem to be anything anyone was alarmed about—that is, no one but me. When the coyotes were howling and answering each other, I used to wonder what would happen if my legs wouldn't carry me home. First there would be a lot of howling in one direction and then in another. Sometimes it seemed as if they were surrounding me, and I would get a little scared as the evening darkened and I had to get the sheep to the corral for the night. I always had my dog with me and I felt a little more secure with him. Still, old bulls that had been turned loose on the range were in that area too, and I had to watch for rabid coyotes and rattlesnakes. When you are a child and walking a long way from home, every little thing seems a danger.

✢

WHEN I WAS STILL QUITE A SMALL CHILD, we leased summer pasture high on Steens Mountain. Our cabin was among a bunch of quaking aspen trees with a grassy patch around it and a creek running down beside it. I was probably only six or seven the last time we lived there, but the memories are still vivid for me because it was one of the most beautiful places in my life.

It was twenty-five miles from our house in the foothills to the cabin on the top of the Steens, and we used a team and wagon to move up for the summer. It took us one whole day to make the trip to the cabin. When I was still small, I rode in the alforja with a load of camp stuff in the other side to balance. An alforja is a canvas bag with leather straps to hold it solid and leather loops to hang on the X's on each end of the wooden packsaddle. The word is Spanish for saddlebag—the Spanish were the first Europeans in the area a long time ago, and they left a lot of horses. That's where some of the wild mustangs come from that still roam the area today. If the load on the other side of the horse was too heavy, Dad put a rock in my side to balance the load. When my little brother John came along, we both rode in the alforjas, one on each side of the same horse. After my sister was born, when there were three children, I had to ride on the horse with the baby Kathleen in one bag and John in the other. It was a wide spread for a little girl's legs behind the packsaddle. Later they harnessed the team to the wagon and I got to ride the saddle horse.

With the wagon we had to take two days to make the trip, trailing the sheep, and we would camp on the way up at V Lake. It was beautiful there, and the lake was full of water lilies, with deer eating around the edge. The only bad thing was that the mosquitoes at night came in swarms. We had bedrolls on the ground for sleeping, and we had to cover our heads to keep from being eaten. As we got older, Mom and

Dad took their mattress up the mountain and put it on the wooden bed frame that Dad made. The frame was made of juniper posts, and it was high enough that a little cot could fit under it for my brother and me. The cabin was small, but we spent most of our time outdoors.

ONCE A WEEK WHILE WE STAYED at the Steens cabin, either Mom or Dad would ride down to the ranch to check on Grandma and to go to Fields for supplies. One day Mom had left for supplies and had put a cardboard box of dirty clothes out by the creek, where she was going to wash them with her washboard. She had tied the box up in the branches of a tree by the creek to keep out the bugs. It was dark when we heard a rustling in the tree, and Dad got out the gun because he said he could hear a porcupine chewing on the box of clothes. We didn't have a light of any kind to go out and look so he took his rifle and shot towards the noise. Everything was quiet and we went back to sleep.

The next morning when we went out to see if the clothes were damaged, sure enough, there was a dead porcupine and a hole in the box. Dad took the box down and emptied it on the ground and we checked to see if anything was chewed. Nothing had been ruined, but Dad found a nightgown of Mom's and he tossed it over his head and danced around, entertaining us. We thought it was hilarious and we were in hysterics when we heard laughing behind us. We didn't expect any company, but there were three buckaroos on horses, sitting on their horses and whooping it up. Dad ran for the bushes, took off the nightgown, and when he came out, he tried to look like nothing had happened.

DAD WAS USUALLY A PRETTY GOOD COOK, but we were always glad when Mom came back. She would carry our week's supplies in one gunnysack tied to the saddle, which amazes me today when I come home from the grocery store with sack after sack in the car. Sometimes we ate watercress and another weed we called Willy

Britches, which grew under the sagebrush. We put sugar and vinegar on these greens for a salad. If there was a good rain, we all headed out to places where we knew the mushroom and puff balls would spring up like magic. Mom cooked them with bacon and they were very good.

I LOVE STEENS MOUNTAIN. I love it today and as a little child I loved it. It was cool there, and there were so many birds: mountain bluebirds, meadowlarks, magpies, golden eagles. Of course, there were animals and so many shrubs and trees that we didn't have down on the other ranch. Mom dug holes in the bottom of the creek running past the cabin for her kettles, where she put them to keep the food cool. I would sit on the grassy spot under the trees, Mom would put the flour and water into the sourdough jar, and I got to stir, which seemed like a big deal to a child. When my brother was there too, we would ride the tree limbs as if they were our horses, but we had to look out for the wasp nests. I had a pet bullfrog and when I wanted him, I stomped on the hole where he lived and he would come out. Dad had painted Mutt and Jeff on the side of the wagon, and on the front of the cabin he painted Major Hoople. I used to wonder if heaven could be like the Steens.

✦

DAD LOVED TO DRAW and so did I. He was a good artist and would draw on anything; in fact, my mother used to complain that there wasn't a surface in the house on which he hadn't drawn one figure or another. Lots of the figures he drew were really strange characters and mine were too; in fact, many of mine were monsters, and Mom didn't like them at all. "Why do you draw things like that," she would ask, but I didn't know. They just popped into my mind, even when I was a little kid, and it wasn't until I went to Ireland and saw many figures like mine that I knew they came from some sort of ancestral heritage. But I'd draw anything as a child, especially horses and other animals.

I developed an elaborate fantasy world that Mom called my dreamland. I called it Ascripfa, which was just a word I made up, and this dreamland was inhabited by a variety of animals and characters that I drew in great detail. I made up stories about each animal: what it ate, where it lived in the mountains, and what its name was. The name was always some word I had invented. The animals usually had big teeth and resembled dragons. This was in the thirties and there was a scarcity of paper in those days, which is why the day after elections was like Christmas for me.

EVERY YEAR MOM WAS ON the election board at the Red Point School House, which was at the south end of Harney County near Denio, almost twenty-five miles from home. Voting was taken pretty seriously in those days, and practically everyone in the county came, no matter how far it was. The polls were open until eight, and then the ballot box had to be delivered to Burns, a long trip, so the neighbors took turns doing it. We kids got to go and play with the old ballots and the indelible pencils while we waited for the ballots to be counted and then put into the ballot box. Then the ballot box had to be sealed with red melted wax that came in a sort of long pencil form.

When the ballot box was on its way to Burns, Mom and Dad and whoever else was still there stayed to clean the school for the next day. They stayed a long time talking and I think they were glad for the company, as we lived so far apart from each other. Then we kids got to take home all the unused ballots for drawing paper. We got all the unused wax and the indelible pencils too, which were fun to play with because when they got wet they were like ink.

When the school was clean and it was nearly midnight, we still had to drive twenty-five miles of rough road, so of course we kids were asleep by the time we got home. I could hardly wait until the next day to draw to my heart's content. This was like a gift from heaven, and I cherished every sheet and made each one last as long as I could by using every available empty space. I used to dream of living in a huge warehouse full of paper and brand new pencils clear to the ceiling with just little trails to get from one stack of paper to another. That would be the most wonderful place in the world, I thought, and the day after the election was the closest I came to that dream.

I LOVED GOING OUT IN THE HILLS with my dad. I guess when he was in school in Ireland he learned lots of poetry, because he could recite lots of poems and he did that while we were watching the sheep. When he wrote his own poems, he wrote on all kinds of subjects, just whatever was on his mind, even about the sheep. We called him the Rimrock Poet, and to this day I can see his silhouette against the mountain as he sat among the sage and juniper, writing his poems, with a smile on his face as the lines were coming to him.

Lots of sheepherders had their camps up on the mountain in the summer, and in the evening we could see their bonfires. That made for a warm feeling; other people were on the mountain too, taking care of their sheep. We used to try to locate the exact place their camps would be, and sometimes in the daytime we would go for a visit. There was a

mining operation going on up there too, and Dad was interested in that so sometimes we would talk with the miners. Because of Dad's interest in geology, we were always hunting rocks while we were watching the sheep. We would find pieces of fire opal and Indian arrowheads, and Dad would point out cinnabar in some of the rocks, and copper as well. Whenever I was with Dad, it was a continual educational experience.

DAD WAS SIX FEET ONE and they called him Steens Mountain Ben. It was legendary in the county that he could walk faster than a horse, and often he went places on foot because of that. Although he was tall and strong, he was in no way violent; he was a sheep man, not a wild buckaroo who got into fights. Only once did he strike someone. He didn't like killing anything, which was a bit of a problem when we needed meat. Mom would ask him to butcher a sheep, but he would put it off as long as he could. He would catch a fat wether, a castrated male sheep, and say to Mom, "Gosh, Zola, how can I kill the poor little fellow?" Then he'd let it go. A few days would go by and Mom would say, "Ben, we have to have some meat for the children, so you must butcher." Another few days would go by and Dad would come into the house for a meal and Mom would have sardines, not Dad's favorite dish, on the table. Then he would butcher. He just hated killing anything. He could walk among his sheep and they would seldom move or stop eating and he could point his finger at his milk cow and tell her to moo and she would. He would catch a rooster and carry it around in his arms and pet it. "What a pretty bird," he would say, and down he dropped it and walked off. He was a gentle man to whom no one was a stranger.

✣

FROM THE FIRST THROUGH the eighth grades, I went to school in the one-room schoolhouse in Fields. During the worst winter months when the snow was the deepest, we moved down there to stay in a two-room cabin so we wouldn't miss our education. Dad got the hay wagon and the team of horses, loaded the beds and a few necessities, tied the milk cow to the back of the wagon, and brought the saddle horse to scout out the road ahead for deep drifts. We kids thought it was great fun, but I am sure my parents didn't see it as such. We could ride on the wagon or the horse or walk as much of the way as we wanted. The sheep had to be moved to Fields too, and Dad hauled hay he bought during the winter from the Trout Creek ranchers to feed them. We would stay in Fields until most of the snow was gone from the homestead and we could move back up in the mountains again.

FIELDS WAS NOT A VERY BIG town even in those days. The main, two-story building housed a store with a connecting warehouse, a dance hall, and a two-room living area. There was also the one-room school and an old sod house that had once had several rooms. The town well was near a lath and batten house, and everyone packed their water from there. A rock building had once been used as a stagecoach stop during the days of the borax industry. The ruins of the borax mine were not far from Fields, and sometimes our mom would take us there for a picnic. We found pieces of china dishes and silverware. For ten years, from 1892–1902, this was an active industry run by the Rose Valley Borax Company and fueled by imported Chinese workers. They collected the alkali salts formed when the spring runoff evaporated around Borax Lake. About four hundred tons of these salts were boiled down, using sagebrush for firewood, each year the company was open.

The crystals were put into sacks and hauled by twenty mule teams to the nearest railroad in Winnemucca, Nevada. The old vats were still partly there, and we would wade at the edge of the lake where it was cool and shallow.

THE SCHOOL DIDN'T HAVE ANY electricity so our evening events were lit with gas lanterns. Every fall the parents would get together and go up in the mountains to haul wood for the stove. Each morning the teacher's husband or one of the parents or even the teacher herself would go to the school early and build a fire. Sometimes we would have to leave our coats on all day, as the building wouldn't get warm enough. We never thought we were in that bad of a situation, though. We didn't know that other places had big warm school buildings and an indoor area to play when it was too cold to go outside. We always went outside; really, we didn't know what too cold was.

Girls didn't ever wear jeans or slacks to school, but we did wear long underwear and long stockings. Then one year the parents decided to buy a stove that used oil, eliminating the wood cutting and all the fire building, a decision that was approved unanimously by all. What a relief to be able to leave the stove on at night and just turn it up in the morning. We kids would sit around the stove in the morning till it was warm enough to get our desks back in place.

As this was a relatively new appliance for all concerned, no one knew that if the chimney wasn't cleaned periodically there would be a buildup of soot that in turn caused a lack of oxygen to the firebox and plugged the burner. Every so often the stove would blow up, the door would pop open, and the whole place would be black, including us. A good windstorm would sometimes blow down the chimney and cause the same thing, and everyone would be covered with black soot. Then there was a major cleanup to do.

ONE YEAR THERE WERE MORE children, so some stayed about three miles up a canyon at the McDade ranch. The teacher, Lee Armstrong, stayed there too, as there was no other place for her. The owners of the ranch had a small two-wheeled cart and a donkey that they let the teacher and the students use to get to school. The old donkey would come along fine in the mornings but in the evenings he would balk. There wasn't any way he was going to go until they all got out of the cart; then, if they walked, he would follow. The first few times this happened it was funny but then it got to be a real bother, so they discontinued the cart and the donkey was discontinued too. The teacher and the students boarding at the ranch walked the rest of the year. During the gas rationing of World War II we all did a lot of walking.

THE ONE-ROOM SCHOOL NEVER had very many children. The highest count that we ever had when I was in school was thirteen. That was so exciting, because we had enough people to play different kinds of games. We had never had so many friends to play with before, so this year was an exceptionally good one for all of us. There were children in all grades and one teacher for all different levels.

Some of our lessons were illustrated by our drawings. I loved to draw animals and scenery and my girlfriend loved to draw people, so she and I would work together on our lessons. I think the whole school learned more that way as we all talked about each other's lessons and looked at the drawings. We had to explain them to the others as well as to the teacher. By the time we had gone over the history or whatever we were illustrating, we had repeated it so many times that we pretty well knew it and so did everyone else, no matter what grade they were supposed to be in.

Recess was outdoors most of the time. When we had enough kids, we would play anti-over and pom-pom pull-away but you needed lots of kids for those games. In the wintertime when there was snow on the ground, we played fox and geese and made snow men and snow fairies and had snowball fights. In warmer weather we played baseball, tag, and hide-and-seek in the sagebrush. There were lots of good places to hide under some of the real tall bushes if you beat them first to make sure there were no rattlesnakes. Sometimes the sage grew as high as a man on horseback.

THERE WAS A HILL BY THE SCHOOL that was so much fun we called it the magical hill. It wasn't a really big hill but it was quite steep. In the nice weather it was a great place to race to the top and to see who could run down the fastest. We did high jumps and broad jumps on the flat space at the bottom of the hill. We jumped sagebrush and anything that gave us a challenge. In the winter we would roll big snowballs down the hill and anchor them on the trail in several places. These acted as jump offs for our sleds as we lay on our stomachs and flew down the hill and into outer space. We had to pull the sled up to the top and give the next one a turn. The ones waiting got into throwing snowballs at the one zipping by on the sled and they also got into throwing snowballs at each other.

IN THE LONG DARK WINTER evenings my dad would tell stories for all the schoolkids in the neighborhood. We had to sit on the floor as there was no room for chairs in that little cabin at Fields, so I can't say that the stories left us sitting on the edge of our chairs, but each night left us eager for the next night's story. All the kids loved my dad and I was proud that he was my father.

ONE YEAR WE BUILT A ROCK HOUSE for the teacher and her husband. Our teacher that year was the wife of an English man, Sonny Hollis, who came over from England in the early 1920s. At first Sonny and the teacher lived in the two rooms that were joined to the old dance hall. Then they decided to build themselves a stand-alone house on the property next to the store and across the street. In the evenings after school, the children all came over to help Sonny haul rocks from the side hill next to the building site. We kids thought ourselves essential to this project and we were proud to see the headway each day. In our lives anything anyone did that we could be part of was exciting indeed. Of course there weren't any modern facilities in this house; just a well with a pitcher pump, kerosene light, and the outhouse, also called the One Hundred Yard Dash.

AFTER THE HOUSE WAS BUILT, Sonny and Lucille, and Sonny's mother and brother, moved in. This was a small four-room house. The mother and brother shared a bedroom and Sonny and Lucille shared one. As time progressed Sonny decided he wanted a shop to work on cars and fix tires, so he built a metal building to use as his garage-workshop. Sonny's brother was blind, and his mother was nearly blind from old age. Sonny tied a rope from the back door of the living room to the outhouse so the brother and the mother could use the facilities without help getting back and forth. We kids were very pleased with that house.

WE HAD DIFFERENT TEACHERS at the school, and all of them made an impression on me. Once a teacher gave me a box of paints for Christmas and I will never forget opening that gift. The paints were watercolors, and to this very day I can remember the elation that went through my entire body in a physical wave at the sight of such heavenly magic.

Sometimes we didn't even have a teacher at the start of school. When I was in eighth grade a neighbor, Denisie Wenzel, had to teach school for a while and my mother had to substitute. Then one dark night a friend of my parents stopped by our place and told us that he had the new teacher and her daughter out in the car. He didn't stay long as it was getting late and he wanted to get them to their new home.

We were so excited to get to school and see the new people. I found out that the daughter would be in my age group, and that was fantastic. For the first time we had four girls in our grade: Annie, Donna, and I—and now this new girl, a pretty blond named Teddy. The next morning Teddy came to school to meet all of us, and we were thrilled. Her mother didn't come until the next day, and we were not so thrilled then.

The new teacher, Mrs. Kell, got up in front of the room and introduced herself and her daughter. She told us we would have a morning ritual where we pledged allegiance to the flag, sang "God Bless America," and then we were to sit down and she would come around and give the different grades our lessons for the day. She told us right off that she would not permit any foolishness and for us all to keep our noses in the books unless she spoke to us or told us otherwise.

This scared me to death. I kept my nose in my book, but I don't remember reading anything. I just sat there wondering what was going to happen next. I looked over at my brother John, and I could see big tears in his eyes. John was always such a tenderhearted kid. You could have heard an ant sneeze in that room. When we went out for recess, we didn't know whether we should get too friendly with Teddy or not. Her mom came outside too. We had never been supervised outside before; we had lost our freedom there too. Teddy was a cutie but she sure had a mean mother.

When I went home, I told my mom and dad that I didn't like the new teacher and that she was really mean. Mom said, "Well, you really don't know her yet and I'm sure once we all get acquainted things will be fine." So after school was out the next night, Mom went over and introduced herself and the two ladies talked. When Mom came home, she said that the new teacher was beside herself. She had been told that the kids she was coming to teach were real terrors and were all unmanageable. She was coming from McClaren School in Portland, which was for boys who had gotten in trouble with the law, and she thought it would be like that. But she couldn't believe it when she had given her speech and some of the children had tears in their eyes, and now she was afraid she had made a bad impression on the students.

After that things got better. Teddy seemed to be a friendly, fun girl, and my mom liked her mother so well that they became good friends. Mom didn't have many friends to visit in that part of the country. The other ranch wives were as busy as she was and they all lived a long way apart. After a while Mrs. Kell told Mom that the children were all just darling and she didn't know why she had been told they were so bad. She felt she had to scare them to get the upper hand first. We loved Teddy and had ever so much fun during the year after all.

FOR ONE THING WE HAD a great school carnival that year. Each year we held a carnival to make money for the school, and we all had a booth. We had a fish pond, a dart game, a horseshoe-throwing booth, a roulette wheel, all sorts of things. My booth was the kissing booth. For five cents you could buy a candy kiss, and I was selling lots of them, but then one man wanted the real kind and it was confusing for me. This was a friend of my Dad's, and he was usually a very nice man, but he'd had a little too much to drink and wouldn't give up. I escaped out the back under the sheet we had hung up for the booth. After that I had a fortune-telling booth with cards.

THAT YEAR MRS. KELL DECIDED that we should have a little musical band. As we did not have much money for instruments, we decided to buy ukuleles, which were $1.49 from the Montgomery Ward catalog. We practiced and practiced on a lot of songs until we thought we were pretty good. Our mothers made pale blue and white pinafores with white satin blouses for the girls; the boys wore blue corduroy pants and white shirts. Every time there was a community meeting, we had to perform. We sang too: "Deep in the Heart of Texas," "You Are My Sunshine," "Red River Valley," and many others. Our entertainment was a lot of work for us and, most of all, for the teacher. She had to plan and work on us for the next month ahead. The parents really enjoyed our efforts, though, and we were well rewarded with lots of clapping and sometimes even a standing ovation. We thought we were really good.

THESE COMMUNITY MEETINGS were once a month, and they were for school business and anything else that needed the attention of the community. First the business meeting was held, and then the schoolchildren provided some entertainment, like the ukulele band, and after that there was always a dance. These meetings were held in the evenings so all could attend, and everyone did: the ranchers, the buckaroos, and the Irish and Basque sheepherders who camped in the lower elevations for the winter. Locals who mostly played by ear provided music for the dance. Jimmy McDade had a banjo and guitar and sometimes other musicians would come. There was usually someone to play the piano and sometimes the accordion. Our meetings were always held in the dance hall, as it was the only place big enough for us all.

At midnight the dance stopped and the ladies, who always brought lots of food, served the meal. My folks took us home as they said things were going to get a little wild after that. Some danced till daylight and then they went home, did the chores, and came back and danced some more. Those buckaroos and the sheepherders who came up from the desert knew how to have a good time.

SOMETIMES EVERYONE HAD too good of a time. Once after a dance a Basque sheepherder named Angel had passed out beside the dance hall, and he was still there come late afternoon the next day, so some of us kids decided he was dead. I don't remember why none of the grown-ups had seen him, but we knew that when animals died, we buried them. None of us had actually seen a dead person, but this man looked to us like he needed burying, so we all got shovels and dug a trench beside him. It wasn't a very deep trench, because the ground was hard, but we did the best we could. We lined it with gunnysacks and rolled him into it, and he happened to land faceup. We covered him with more gunnysacks, and my brother decided that just in case he might not be clear dead we had better put a piece of stovepipe over his face before we covered him entirely. We started at his feet and began covering him with dirt while my brother arranged the stovepipe. Just then, here came some of the parents, and they wanted to know what we were doing. We told them the man was dead and we were burying him.

Needless to say, they got the man out of the hole and he began to come to and was he ever scared. We got a talking to and they helped the fellow over to the porch of the store and sat him down there. He was still not his normal self but after a day or two he went home, leaving his convertible Model T behind him. That was another mistake.

Anything that looked abandoned turned into a toy for us kids. Soon we had discovered that this Model T was really light and we could push it around. So we pushed it up the hill and we all jumped in. My brother steered down the hill and around the store we came. We made it clear across the little bridge and coasted as far as we could down the road. If anyone had been coming from the south it could have been a disaster all the way around, but kids don't think like that, of course. Like always, the parents stepped in again and put a stop to our fun and we got another talking to.

All of us knew better than to bother other people's property, but we did it anyway. I guess we thought that man wasn't going to make it so we might as well have a little fun with his car. It was a disappointment to us when he returned for the car and drove off in it. But we did take it all in when he got out the crank and cranked it till it started. "Now we'll know how to start it next time he comes to town and we won't have to push it," my brother said. But this was one sheepherder that didn't do his drinking in Fields anymore. I guess he felt lucky to be able to leave alive—he almost didn't.

✢

MY CHILDHOOD WAS FILLED with various wild critters. I've already mentioned the snakes, which were a constant factor. We children were taught to always carry a long stick and beat the brush in front of us for rattlesnakes. We learned the lesson well because rattlesnakes were just a fact of life in the high desert where we lived; I've never gotten over my fear of them. We had to watch out for them all the time around the house and especially out herding the sheep. They occasionally would bite the sheep's noses, but the sheep's wool protected them and usually they would run when they heard the rattle. Rattlesnakes in our part of the country were diamondbacks but the bull snakes have colorful backs too, and it's hard to tell which one it is unless you can see its tail.

Once I looked up at the bedroom ceiling and there was a snake coiled around the rafter. "Snake!" I yelled, every bit as loud as Jerry Murphy had yelled when the snake came out of the root cellar, and Dad came running. Even he couldn't tell what kind of snake it was when it was curled that way; we couldn't see the tail. Rattlesnakes have at least one rattle and more as they get older; bull snakes have a long thin pointed tail. Dad grabbed the broom and pushed me out of the room. In fact, he made us all get out of the house because he didn't want any mad rattlesnake falling on our heads. This one turned out to be a bull snake and after Dad got it coiled around the broom, he tossed it out of the house.

You don't kill bull snakes just to kill them. The old story was that where there was a bull snake there wouldn't be a rattler. We had another big bull snake that lived near the shallow reservoir by the road and we didn't bother him either. He took up residence under an apple crate we used as part of a raft. We didn't mind the bull snakes; we figured we'd rather deal with a bull snake than to have to fend off a rattler. But the rattlesnakes weren't as bold as the coyotes. Those coyotes were plenty bold, even when they weren't rabid.

Even regular coyotes that weren't sick would come into the chicken pen to steal chickens. They weren't at all afraid of the barking dogs and they'd grab a hen and be long gone before my dad could get out there with the gun. I guess they came after the chickens when they got tired of rabbits, and when they got tired of chickens they would come after the lambs, mostly at night but sometimes in broad daylight.

ONCE WHEN I WAS BRINGING the lambs back to the ranch in the evening, a coyote grabbed a lamb right in front of me. I was riding Coltie, the horse that belonged to the kids, and my dog was with me, but the coyote didn't care. At first I thought this animal must be rabid to be so bold and it even went through my mind that I'd better head for home and get my dad. You don't leave your sheep that way when they've been assigned to your care, so of course I stayed. But that coyote scared me all right the way it circled and circled my little flock of lambs. The dog circled too, barking and barking, trying to keep it away from the sheep.

The coyote just ignored the barking. I was close enough to see it now and I could tell it wasn't sick, just bold. Maybe it had pups of its own at home to feed and it had duty on its mind, just like me. It looked from the dog to me, and when I dismounted to pick up some good-sized rocks to put in my lunch bag, it moved behind the sage, but it didn't go away. I picked up a gnarled juniper limb and got back on my horse, and the coyote moved out in the open again to resume its circling of the sheep. My dog snarled and barked but the coyote paid him no mind, as it had picked out one of the smallest lambs for the kill.

All of a sudden it leaped and had the lamb by the neck. The dog went into frenzied attack but the coyote never even turned. I rode the skittish horse right at it but the coyote wouldn't give up the lamb. I threw my rocks at it too, and one hit it square in the neck, but it still wouldn't let go. I wouldn't necessarily recommend this next course of action, but I was only thinking of saving the lamb.

I jumped off my horse and started beating the coyote with the juniper stick as hard as I could. This may not have been the smartest thing to do—animals can be unexpectedly fierce when defending their food—but my mind was on a single track of protecting my sheep. I whaled away the best I could with the dog nipping at the coyote and getting in my way. Even then the coyote held on for a minute before it finally dropped the lamb, which miraculously was still alive. The coyote slunk away behind the brush, but the whole time I righted the lamb and got my little band together again I felt it was still watching us. I was lucky to get that lamb safely home.

MOST OF THE WILD ANIMALS weren't dangerous. But we lived in a dangerous environment with different kinds of danger than kids face today. We were warned to look out for animals that were acting strangely, and one other time after the drinking water episode we had a rabid coyote come around the house. The folks saw it outside and Dad shot it. We did have porcupines, and the dogs would get tangled up with them and come home with their noses full of quills. The badgers were cute little creatures, but we had to watch out for them because they were real fighters and if you came upon them without warning they would bite. Their holes weren't easy to see when you were running through the brush. Sometimes we would see bobcats up by the rimrock or coyote puppies by their dens, and we knew the mother wasn't far away. Daily we saw deer. Some kind of wildlife always seemed to be lurking in the bushes and often it felt like something was watching us. That wasn't really a scary feeling; most of the wildlife, even the rattlesnakes, was more wary of us than we were of it. High on the hills we could see wild horses.

✛

WE HAD WILDLIFE PETS that sometimes caused trouble, like the horny toads. Horny toads aren't so much toads as a species of lizard. They're small—some get as big as a fifty-cent piece—with three little horns and a ruffled edge all around them. They can be tethered by looping a string behind their front legs and making a sort of harness. They come in different colors, mostly tan and gray. We kids each had our own toads. We would paint the horns with different colors of nail polish so we knew which one belonged to which of us. We made little pens with coffee cans, adding a bit of dirt, a few rocks, a sprig or two of sagebrush, and some grass for them to hide under. We put in a jar lid with water, and then it was up to us to find flies because that's mostly what they wanted to eat. One we kept tied to Mom's geranium, which was in a pot sitting on the windowsill. This was so he could have access to the flies that ventured in. We took him down to Fields with us when we moved there in the winter. The Fields cabin was very small and the geranium window was directly over the head of the bed. The horny toad got loose and we couldn't find him, which was devastating and all of us kids had a big cry over it.

Several days went by and then one night right after Mom and Dad went to bed and Dad blew out the light, Mom let out a big scream. "There's something crawling up my leg."

"Don't move," said Dad; he probably thought it was a rattlesnake. "All of you stay in your beds and I'll light the light and pull the covers off all at once." Off came the covers. Sure enough, there was the old horny toad. That was the last time horny toads were allowed in the house. We had to put him outside and let him fend for himself.

IN THE WINTERTIME the wild burros would come down to Fields to get handouts during the livestock feeding. The burros seemed to like to be around the schoolkids; they would come over at recess and during the noon hour. One became very gentle and all the school kids loved her. We would lean on her and jump up on our stomachs and hang over her back, and she didn't seem to mind. We decided to name her and we put letters together from everybody's name until we came up with something we could pronounce. We called her Japeglatara. When spring came the burros headed back into the green grass of the mountains. That's when we really knew summer was coming and school would soon be out.

ANOTHER TIME IN FIELDS an orphan deer that didn't like men or boys came to the school. She hated the dogs too and would try to stomp them with her sharp hooves. She had only one horn but she was wicked with it when she wanted to be. But she loved us girls, and she liked to be petted and scratched. She became such a problem with the boys that eventually the men caught her, took her up on the mountain, and turned her loose. Later we were told that as a tiny fawn she had been literally cut out of her mother, who had been shot and butchered by a hunter. When she was found, she was almost dead, lying by the innards of her mother. I don't know why the coyotes didn't get her, but the rancher took her home and his family raised her. But when she got mean, they took her up on the mountain, and that's when she found her way over to the town and came to the school. After the men in Fields took her away, we never saw her again.

WE HAD ANOTHER LITTLE DEER we named Cleopatrick. This was at the homestead ranch. One day late in the fall after hunting season, one of the sheep men came down from the mountains with his pack string for supplies. The sheep men would ride their horses down to our place, where they had left their vehicles. That way they had a place to stay overnight and a chance to visit. This sheep man had a baby deer on his packsaddle snuggled in the alforja. The mother had been shot and had died, which left the baby to die or to be eaten by other wild animals. The fawn was real hungry and wouldn't have lasted much longer without food. It was brown and still covered with white spots. We fed her Mother's Rolled Oats and milk and nicknamed her Cleo. She soon learned her name and made a funny little noise when we called her. She followed us everywhere we went. We put a red ribbon around her neck so she would be identified and no one would shoot her. We had lots of wild pets, but as they grew up they usually went their own way.

A LOT OF ROMANCE IS attached to wild horses today, but when I was a child they were really wild animals, not just pets to be tamed. The herds on the Steens are descended from horses brought by the Spanish and the real mustangs have a black stripe down their spine. They are beautiful animals with thick, wavy manes and tails that are so long they sometimes drag on the ground.

My dad loved horses, and he had a lot of them. Some he bought from the company ranches over around Roaring Springs, way back in the late twenties and thirties. (The big spreads were mostly company ranches, owned by some rich outfit in California or maybe even New York. These companies would buy ranches and hire someone to run them, and they would fly in to check on things every so often. Roaring Springs Ranch, Three Mile Ranch, Home Creek Ranch, and H.L. Ranch were all company ranches. They worked their wells for irrigation using gasoline motors until about 1957, when the REA got electricity there.) The horses from these ranches, which we called the Cannon Ball breed, came from Australia and they, like the mustangs, were not large, but they were sturdy and sure-footed.

These Australian horses mixed with the other horses Dad owned. In the months that we didn't need them for working the sheep, most of them were put out to range for themselves in the mountains and they mixed with the mustangs too. This was fine with Dad. When we walked to the top of the mountains looking for our horses, we used to see bands of wild mustangs, but my dad warned us to stay away from them. Having almost been killed by one, he wasn't so romantic about mustangs.

THE STALLIONS IN WILD HORSE herds are mean and protective. They don't just go after other stallions; they'll attack anything that might be threatening to their mares. One day Dad went up the mountains to get some of our horses and saw a band of mustangs not too far away from where our horses were grazing. He didn't want to tangle with them. Our horses were closer to him, so Dad decided to try to attract them by using their natural curiosity. This was a trick he had used before to catch the horses, and it worked because the horses couldn't resist investigating anything that looked strange. He tied his white handkerchief to his foot, lay down on the ground and waved his foot in the air. Unfortunately, it was not our horses Dad attracted, but the wild stallion, and he was fighting mad.

Dad saw him coming and jumped up and ran. Luckily for him there was a huge boulder nearby, and he scrambled up on it just as the stallion charged. The horse was squealing, with his ears flat on his head and his mouth open. He was raking at Dad with his front feet and if he had caught him it would have been all over. The trouble was that the boulder wasn't quite high enough for Dad to be safe from the horse.

The wild stallion kept circling the boulder; sometimes he would rear up and put his forelegs on the rock like he was going to climb right up there with Dad. Dad wasn't sure that the stallion couldn't actually do it—those mustangs were used to climbing on all sorts of uneven terrain. All Dad could do was scramble from one side of the rock to the other side, trying to keep out of range of the hooves and teeth. He kicked at the horse's face, but he was afraid of losing his balance; he knew if he fell off the boulder his life would be over. The stallion would pummel him until he was dead. This went on literally for hours with that wild horse charging around the rock and Dad scrambling frantically from one side to the other to avoid him. Dad was near exhaustion by the time the stallion finally gave up and went back to his herd. He waited until the horse was a long way away, and then he made a hasty escape over the rimrock and ran down the mountain to our home.

DAD HAD MORE THAN HIS SHARE of encounters with dangerous wild things: coyotes, mustangs, even birds. Once he came practically crawling home, dragging his leg, which was entirely covered with blood, his pants leg almost ripped off. This time it was a golden eagle that almost got him. Taylor Grazing, the government agency that later became the Bureau of Land Management, came around and set traps for coyotes that were killing sheep. Sometimes Dad set traps too, if our lambs had been disappearing, so I don't know exactly who set this one. A golden eagle, attracted by the dead lamb that had been left for bait, got its leg snared in the trap. Dad tried to get the eagle out, but the eagle got him instead. These are huge birds with a wingspan of over seven feet, and this one was terrified, of course, and it sunk its other talon right around Dad's knee. Then Dad was stuck too; finally it was either him or the eagle, and he had to wring its neck. Even with the bird dead, he had to cut off the eagle's leg with his pocketknife because he couldn't remove the talons from where they were curved around his kneecap. Mom had to finish the job for him after he limped and crawled home.

✢

OF COURSE THE MOST IMPORTANT animals for us were the sheep. Even before Mom and Dad were married, Dad had built up his own band. This was during the Great Depression and money was hard to come by and even harder to keep. One year on the ranch when I was still pretty small, the bank took the sheep. When I asked Mom what happened, she said that there wasn't enough money that year. The hired hands wanted paying and the bank wanted paying too, so Dad paid the workers and had to give up the sheep to the bank.

THAT WAS A BAD YEAR all around, the same year a range fire started up high on the west side of the Steens by the road at the top of Long Hollow. The story later was that it must have been a cigarette because there hadn't been any lightning storms for a strike; that's the way range fires usually started. The first we kids knew about it was when Dad came running into the house, yelling for Mom to get us because the whole mountain above the house was on fire.

Range fires are unpredictable and hard to control; the dry grass is just like kindling and if the fire gets going good, it generates its own wind power. Sometimes it goes so fast that it burns around the brush and trees and stays on the ground. But once it's really hot, nothing in its path is safe; trees, animals, houses, people all get burned, and the wind can make it shift directions with one breath.

The CCC (Civilian Conservation Corps) boys were camped over at the northern mouth of Long Hollow, and they had trucks with water tanks. They filled tubs with water for Mom and Dad to dip gunnysacks in and they gave us kids drinks of water, but they didn't help the folks beat the fire back from the house. They took pictures of us and one even had some kind of movie camera, but they didn't help; I have no idea why. We kids were scared to death and we carried the wet gunnysacks back and forth to Mom and Dad. Just when we thought we had lost the house for sure, the wind shifted the fire to the east and it headed down the mountain toward Andrews. That is the only time I ever saw my dad collapse from exhaustion, but he and Mom had saved the house. The fire burned several more days before it went out. The bank had already taken the sheep, so at least none of them burned in the fire.

BUT DAD WENT BROKE. I was too young then to understand what that must have meant to them, but I know now that this was a devastating time in their lives. They kept the homestead ranch and for a while they ran the small hotel at Fields, which had been empty. Mom did all the cooking at the hotel, and Dad hired out to others. He worked for the county, grading the roads with a four-horse-drawn grader. A black man, a neighbor from the Trout Creek area, worked with him. He drove the horses while Dad manipulated the grader blade.

Dad also worked in the hay fields in the summer, which was definitely dangerous work because you were always faced with the very real prospect of getting killed. Horses were the only way to pull the machines and these horses were pretty undependable. Most of them had been turned loose to run wild on the range to forage when they weren't used, and they had to be rounded up and caught in corrals when they were needed for work. If enough men could get a horse caught, harnessed, and hooked to a mower or rake, they could use it. Then it was up to the man operating the machine to hang on until the wild horses were tired enough to manage. It was nothing to see a man zipping across the rough fields at several miles an hour, bouncing in the air and trying to hang on for all he was worth. If the man fell off, it could be the end of him, so this was literally a matter of life and death. This was the way the horses were broken, and by the end of the summer the horses were gentle and manageable. Dad had some narrow escapes and was hurt several times, but luckily he wasn't killed like some of the men. When he got some money together he bought more sheep.

WITH SHEEP RANCHING there were definite seasons with different kinds of work. In the winter the sheep were penned and fed hay, cottonseed, and molasses cubes so the ewes would stay in good shape for the lambing. Most of the time, weather and grass permitting, the sheep were taken out on the hillsides to drop their lambs. This was early in April, and it was absolutely musical to hear the bleating of the new lambs and the comforting soft answers of the mothers. During lambing season out on the range, the sheep were separated into the dry bunch with the bucks, and the separate herd with the ewes and their lambs. The ewes and lambs couldn't travel around as much till the lambs got strong.

After shearing the bucks were taken out and put on pasture separate from the rest until fall, and they needed a herder to watch them. I loved being outdoors and I loved the smell of the wildflowers and juniper and the excitement of cooking on the little camp stove—outside the tent if the weather permitted and inside if it didn't. These stoves were tin and very light. They had small chimney pipes and beside the fire box there was a little oven for fresh baked sourdough biscuits that would be served with honey and jam. We sat on rocks outside the tent and held our plates on our laps, but we didn't sit on the sacks of salt. We always had several sacks of salt at camp for the sheep. When they started eating brush you knew they wanted salt. But I must warn you, don't ever sit on a sack of rock salt because it will make you itch.

The sheep were usually through lambing by May or around the first of June, and we did the shearing then. When Dad was building up his band after the Depression, he did all the shearing himself with the help of the family. When he had an even bigger band—he got his band up to two thousand sheep—we took them over to Jimmy McDade, who had a shearing corral. But that was later—for several years we did it ourselves. Dad had a pair of hand shears (like a pair of scissors only shaped a little differently) and after he got more sheep than he could shear by hand, he got a little gas motor and an electric shears. When we did our own shearing, my brother and I had to keep the pen full so he could drag out one sheep after another.

The wool had to be packed in big sacks about eight feet long, and you could get several fleeces in one sack if they were tromped down. The sack was hung up in a special wooden tower with a big round steel ring, and the wet top of the sack was stretched around this ring. The fleeces were put in the sack one at a time after Mom had tied them with fleece string; each fleece had to be compressed as much as possible. My little brother would get right in the wool sack and layer the wool, tromping it down as best he could. Sometimes Mom would get in the sack and tromp too, but to finish it up Dad would get in. Then the sack was let down off the tower and sewed with twine across the end, and it was ready to put on the truck and send to market. Most of our wool went to the scouring mills in Portland where it was dispersed to different factories.

ONCE WHEN WE WERE STILL doing our own sheep, it was just Mom and Dad, John, me, and little Kathleen, and we had all been working since early in the morning and were already quite tired. About noon Mom said, "Why don't you and John run over and get some dinner together for us?" We were glad to do it to get out of the dusty corral. We had to build our sagebrush fire and get the stove hot first, and we decided that we would bake a cake to go with dinner. Mom had a recipe for a one-egg cake that was pretty easy, so we whipped it together while we were waiting for the stove to get hot.

Then we decided to add a little spice to our lives by putting the batter into the bread pan and using food coloring to make it look pretty. We put in swirls of blue, red, green, and yellow and it looked beautiful. We were just going to pop it in the oven to bake while we heated up the rest of the dinner when we noticed that the egg was still on the table. Well, we knew the cake would all crumble without the egg, so there was nothing to do but beat up the egg and stir it in. The cake batter turned a muddy color and looked an awfully lot like dirt. So we dumped in a huge gob of blue coloring and stirred it up again. That looked pretty good, a nice bright blue, so we baked it and got it all frosted with powdered sugar frosting. Then we put it on Mom's fancy cake plate and put it in the middle of the table.

Just as Mom and Dad and Kathleen came in to eat, here came Jerry Murphy, the Irishman with the bushy eyebrows and red hair who'd been so scared of the snake in the cellar, so of course we set another plate. John and I never said a word about the cake. When all had finished eating their dinner, I got a knife to cut the cake and put the first piece on a little plate and handed it to our company.

Jerry's bushy eyebrows shot right up into his already straight-up red hair. "Ha!" he said like a clap of thunder, and then, "Oh, Jesus Christ!" You'd have thought another snake had crawled between his legs; for a second I thought he was going to go tearing down the hill, thinking that we had tried to poison him.

But he didn't. He ate the cake, and it was quite good, so we gave him another piece. Mom and Dad didn't want to hurt our feelings but I could tell they were trying not to laugh when Dad said the cake was very tasty. After that we told them the story of the egg, and we all had a good laugh with Jerry as well. Jerry stayed and helped us and we finished up the shearing that afternoon. It was always even more fun to work when he was around; he got into those big sacks and stomped like the wild man he was.

AFTER THE SHEARING WAS DONE, it was time to head for the summer pastures with the sheep. Sheep herding might seem like a lazy job to those who don't know the difference, but it's not; it's very tiring with lots of walking and horseback riding involved. All the sheep were on the range during the summer months so they could eat bunch grass and browse, and they needed to be watched at all times to keep them together and safe from coyotes and bobcats. The sheep like to pull the bed ground at a very early hour, at daylight, so you have to be ready to go when they are. This can wear out a lot of shoes even if you have a horse.

WE KNEW A HERDER ONCE named Arthur who wore out his shoes and couldn't get to Burns to get any more. He cut up some old tires and tied them onto his old shoes, but that didn't work either. The store at Fields always carried a few pair for just such emergencies. None of them fit this Irishman, so he took a pair of cowboy boots as that was the only thing left. He tried everything to make those boots work, even chopping down the heels, which nearly ruined his legs. So they sent a radio message to JCPenney at Burns to send down some shoes on the stage.

The stage was a pickup truck that ran from Burns to Denio. It went south on Monday and north on Tuesday; south on Wednesday and north on Thursday; south on Friday and north on Saturday. The stage went from Burns to Crane to Fields and then to Denio. It was an all-day trip and it stopped at each little store to deliver the mail and anything that had been ordered. Sometimes we kids got to visit relatives that way, and my mom would talk to the stage driver so he would bring his children too. It was a social lifesaver for isolated kids, but for this sheepherder it was more of a foot-saver. Finally he got some shoes that fit.

YOU JUST HAD TO HAVE good shoes if you were herding sheep, because they moved around a lot and you had to follow. If it was hot they bedded down for the noontime; once it began to cool, they were off eating again. That's when the coyotes liked to come for dinner, so you had to chase the wandering sheep back into the band. My dog did a lot of this for me. Our dogs were highly trained and they were a must for the sheep business. They were awfully smart about finding the sheep and would even stand on their hind legs to look for sheep that might have strayed from the band and bedded down behind bushes. If they found an injured sheep we couldn't see, they stayed there and barked until we came to get the sheep.

There were always a certain number of bells in a band of sheep, and if a bell sheep was missing, you knew that there were more sheep missing that you had to hunt for. Another marker was a black sheep. For every so many sheep you would have one black one so you could

figure out whether you had all your sheep by just counting the blacks.
You had to know where your sheep were at all times and watch for any
quick movements that might indicate trouble and start them running:
a coyote, a jackrabbit jumping from the brush, a sage grouse, or even a
rattlesnake. All of these things had to be investigated and if there was
trouble, you had to be able to deal with it.

ONCE MY BROTHER AND I were out with the sheep, and it was
almost dark when we found one with blind staggers. That's when a sheep
eats some kind of poison root like larkspur and gets totally disoriented
and keeps falling down. We couldn't leave her there, several miles from
home, or a coyote would eat her for sure, so we had to put her on the
horse. Coltie had been tamed from the wild by a neighbor, and we kids
had broken her to ride. Now, this little horse never had a sheep on her
before, but we got that sick sheep up on the saddle.

This sheep was too heavy for one of us alone to lift, but we both got
her partway on the saddle on one side and then John got on the other
side and got her two front legs while I had her balanced on my knee.
John pulled and I pushed and we got to giggling, but we got her up on
the saddle all right. Then we tied her up there. On the way down the
hill to the corral I went ahead and John walked behind to make sure she
didn't fall off. If she started to slip, he would yell and I stopped the horse
and we fixed her again. By the time we got to the corral, the moon was
out big and bright.

We were terribly hungry, but the folks had gone to Burns with some
lambs to fatten up on my uncle's grass pasture before they were sent off
to market, so of course there was no dinner. They had been gone two
days and had taken the baby, but we were left there alone to tend the
sheep. I must have been twelve and my little brother John would have
been nine. We got up at daylight and before we left, we had to build
a sagebrush fire to fry the bacon for our sandwiches. That's what we
always took to eat for lunch; bacon sandwiches and water in syrup cans

with a little screw-on top. We had to have two cans, one for us and one for the horse. She would drink out of the syrup can too, when we held it up for her. She learned to cup her mouth and lips around the little opening on the can so the water wouldn't spill.

John and I were awfully tired that night. Neither of us had the energy to fix any dinner, so we just opened a can of tomatoes and ate that. When I look back now, I can't imagine anyone leaving two small children to do that much work and take on that much responsibility with the sheep. It wasn't that the folks didn't love us, but somebody had to do it, and we were there. They finally got home in the middle of the night, and we were so sound asleep that they had to bang and bang on the door until finally John got up and let them in.

SOMETIMES DURING SPRING BREAK from school, we kids would take our horses and a tent and watch the drys for Dad. Drys are the ewes that are either too young or too old to have lambs and need to be kept separate during the lambing. One time we were up at camp and a burro from another camp down the road decided to come for a visit. We had cleaned the camp and found some spoiled onions, which we threw out some way from the tent. This burro thought they were delicious and ate all of them. That night was a real bright moonlight night, and the burro wanted to come in our tent. We had knotted the ties and he could only get his head in. He brayed and brayed and his breath nearly suffocated us.

WE ALMOST ALWAYS HAD to cope with some unusual situation that was good for developing the quick-thinking skills. Once when my little sister, Kathleen, and I were camped with the drys and Dad was on the other side of the hill with the ewes and lambs, a big windstorm came up and blew down our tent. The problem was that we had the stove inside with its long chimney pipe going up through the ring in the roof. That pipe was hot, and we had to make some pretty fast moves so the tent didn't burn up. Luckily, it was a thin pipe that cooled down quickly.

My sister and I were there several days and it was a particularly eventful week. During the afternoon when the sheep were down and resting, we could skip over the hill and check in with Dad, but at night we were alone. We must have camped on an unusually large population of mice, because at night a lot of them got in the tent. Kathleen woke up screaming that she had mice in her hair. "Just lie still," I said, "and they'll go away." Finally they did, but later in the night coyote pups were playing outside the tent. We could hear them yipping, but the mother must have been out hunting or the sheep would have started making noise and the dogs would have barked. The pups played and played and we could feel them rolling against the side of the tent.

✠

AT TIMES HERDING CAN BE very lonely work, but I never minded herding, even when I did it alone. I was never really afraid out on the hills with the sheep. Usually I had my dog and a lot of the time Johnny was with me; sometimes little Kathleen would come with us too. I hated working inside and I didn't have to help with the housework when I was out on the hills. I felt free as a breeze and happy.

✠

WE RAISED A BUMMER LAMB that was a merino, a breed of sheep that has tight, fine wool. The horns on the bucks are short and curled a little, and they drop off and are replaced. They can also pack a wallop on a buck with a bad temper, like Honey Bunch. Honey Bunch licked his lips and his tongue darted in and out when he was getting ready to go after somebody, like he did when he went after the Watkins man.

One morning we were eating breakfast and didn't hear the Watkins man drive in. He was a sort of traveling salesman who would bring household products that he wanted to sell, like vanilla or soap or some kind of gadgets for the house. All of a sudden the door burst open and this strange man ran in and jumped up on our davenport, still holding his basket of goodies. Right behind him came Honey Bunch, and there he stood in the doorway, licking his chops and getting ready for the big hit. He kept backing up to get a good running start and he was so excited that he messed on the floor before we finally got him back outside the house. But that buck knew the Watkins man was still in there, so he kept ramming into the door until we finally had to shut him up in the barn. We kids were all in hysterics, but the poor man was in hysterics of a different kind. He said he kept trying to get back in his car, but Honey Bunch kept butting the door closed and wouldn't let him get in. Needless to say, that Watkins man never came back again. Honey Bunch was a great pet for us, but he was death on strangers. Anytime anyone came, here came Honey Bunch, his tongue darting in and out, ready to take them on.

THIS CRAZY BUCK USED TO come to school to see us, and when we wouldn't let him in, he would stand out there butting the door. Then he went to the windows, and he could jump in there if the windows were open, because the windows were tall and went down low to the ground. One day the window was closed and I saw him coming full speed ahead. I got the window opened just in time. I was standing to one side and in he came. He slid clear across the room on the oiled floor and slammed into the other wall.

The teacher couldn't believe her eyes. Seeing her standing there was just too much of a good thing for Honey Bunch, and he decided she was a perfect target. He backed up and in and out went the tongue and he charged full force right up the aisle at her. She was scared out of her wits and ran for her desk. When he hit the desk, she ran for the elevated sandbox where we had set up a history lesson with cardboard figures. She mashed Columbus and the Mayflower and some of the Indians in the little village. The buck composed himself and got his tongue going again and here he came again, full force at the sandbox. By this time we kids were all in fits of hysteria, but the teacher was yelling for us to get him out of there and to do it right now. So we had to take him home and tie him up.

A FEW DAYS LATER when one of the boys had to go to the outhouse and didn't come back, the teacher sent my brother out to see what had become of him. Honey Bunch had come back to school and followed the boy to the outhouse. When my brother went out there, the boy told him that the buck had started butting the door so he held it closed until Honey Bunch finally got tired and lay down against the door. Then the boy couldn't get out.

HONEY BUNCH COULD REALLY MOVE out when he wanted to. He chased kids on their bicycles, trying to give them another boost for good measure, and he was dynamite with the sled. In the wintertime we would take the sled up the hill and put a board behind us with a pillow between us and the board. Honey Bunch would come running as fast as he could and hit us from behind. He'd keep running until he caught up with us again and then wham, we got another boost, until we either tipped over or got away from him. We did this with our wagon too. Our big old collie dog liked riding in the wagon, and Honey Bunch would butt the wagon with the dog in it until the dog jumped out. Then he would get down on his knees and butt the wagon some more. He chased us down the hill on our skis. There wasn't anything that Honey Bunch wouldn't chase.

ONCE WHEN WE KIDS had decided we wanted a really tall Christmas tree, we hiked up the hill with the saw to where there was a big juniper. It was farther away than it seemed in the summer, and the snow was deeper than we thought it would be. Junipers are full of pitch and they have a really hard wood. Once we got started we couldn't stop and go after a smaller tree, as this one would surely die, so we sawed and sawed. At last it came down, but it was too heavy for us to carry. We sawed some more, but we still couldn't lift the tree. Pretty soon Dad came with an ax. He and Mom had watched us with the binoculars through the window, so he knew we needed help, and even he had to chop some more off the tree before he could drag it with a rope. As we got close to the barn old Honey Bunch came running to see what the big green thing was that was coming down the hill. I guess he thought he would have a feast of hay or something because when he smelled it and found out it was just a juniper tree it made him furious. He charged Dad and butted him behind the knees until Dad and the tree were down in the snow and he wouldn't let him get up. We all laughed until we were weak.

ONE YEAR A NEIGHBOR of ours had a leppy calf and no way to raise it and no time, either. A leppy calf is the bovine equivalent of a bummer lamb. He gave me the calf and it became my 4-H project. I named him Ferdinand and he had a white face with red, curly hair, pink ears, and a rough pink tongue. I had a special formula I had to feed him and everything had to be recorded in a book. I would call Ferdinand and no matter where he was, he would answer. I put the packsaddle on him and put the dogs in the alforja and took them for a ride. He would follow us up the mountain on our wildflower adventures and carry our lunch. A lady gave me some old neckties that her husband no longer wanted, and every Sunday I would comb Ferdinand's hair with a little water, which made it wavy and pretty. Some buckaroos came by driving their cattle to Long Hollow to summer pasture, and Ferdinand ran to the road to see all the strange animals. They told me they were going to take him along and for a while they did. Then I yelled "Ferdinand" and he bolted up in the air and gave a loud *Moooo!* He turned and ran as fast as he could to me, kicking up his heels and bucking all the way.

I did such a good job with Ferdinand in 4-H that I won a couple of weeks at a summer school camp for rural kids in Corvallis. It was fun to be around a lot of other girls, but they taught us skills that were my regular chores at home, like how to make light bread. We had two kinds of bread: sourdough that was made in the oven outside and light bread that was made in the kitchen with the stove. I thought that learning to make bread was a waste of time, but after we had the dough made, the teacher said we were going to do some fancy things. She rolled it out with the rolling pin, and I thought she was going to make cinnamon rolls, but she didn't. She cut the dough into long strips and braided them and made all kinds of fancy shapes.

When I got home I guess I was feeling my oats, because the first time Mom made light bread and brought it to the table, I piped up and said that I had learned how to make all kinds of fancy things with the dough for light bread, not just the same old loaf or buns. Every one got very quiet at the table, because of course it sounded like I thought I knew more about baking bread than Mom did and that I was saying her bread wasn't any good. Dad looked at me sternly.

"Eileen," he said, "as soon as you get through eating, you go into the kitchen and you make a big batch of light bread and you make it into all kinds of fancy shapes."

Dad never criticized or disciplined us, but when he said something that even implied that we had been bad, it almost broke our hearts. I knew he was angry with me and I could barely finish my food. When I was done I went into the kitchen and stirred up a batch of bread with big tears rolling down my cheeks the whole time. I braided the dough into loaves so we had fancy light bread all right, but I never, ever again said anything about Mom's cooking.

SOMETIMES OUR PETS DIDN'T WORK out the way we had planned. Black Beauty was supposed to be my horse, but it didn't end up that way. One bunch of our horses stayed just over the rim of the Rincon, which was what we called the big bowl at the top of the rimrock, and sometimes they would come down over the lip and we could see them from the house. We could always tell them from the wild bands because there were several that stood out from the rest: my mom's black and white pinto for one; also the all-white mare, the red mule, and the black mule. The rest were mostly bays, with the exception of Black Beauty. He was majestic, shiny, and had a heavy mane and tail. His mane was so thick that it parted on both sides of his neck. It hung down over his eyes and he had to toss his head to see.

Dad taught him to shake hands as a colt, and the only way we could catch him was to yell, "Shake hands," at him, and he would stop and lift his foreleg until we got close enough to shake with him. Then we could slip the rope around his neck. Dad hired a man to break him for me to ride, but he was so spirited that the folks were afraid to let me on him. I wanted to ride that horse more than anything in the world, but he was too wild and I was just a skinny little girl. So Dad loaned him to a friend of his named Billy. I cried but I knew they were afraid I'd get killed, and I also knew that Billy would take good care of him and that he'd bring him by to see me.

One day during the war a man came to our house and offered Dad $300 for that gorgeous black horse. He said he was buying horses for the army and that was the most beautiful horse he had ever seen. Three hundred dollars was a lot of money then, and I'm sure my folks could have used it. I cried and cried because it upset me to think of Black Beauty being shot or wounded and then destroyed, for we knew that could happen to horses in the army. But Dad said no, the horse wasn't for sale, and then he gave him to Billy. Many times Billy would come by with his pack string, so I got to see Black Beauty a lot, and Billy was proud of his beautiful horse.

SOME OF OUR WORK ANIMALS weren't exactly our pets but they had rather distinct personalities, like Johnny the mule. In the spring Dad would grade the road that led from the homestead to Long Hollow to smooth it out, and he used the old county grader. For that he needed a four-horse team, so he borrowed one team from the neighbor and used our team as well. In those days neighbors would help each other out and share animals that might be needed for a chore. Our team was a big brown horse named Buster and Johnny, the big black mule. Buster was a gentle old horse with one bad habit. Every now and then he took a notion to run and he would get all the rest of them running with the equipment, which was a dangerous situation.

Old Johnny-mule had his own quirks. I don't know how that mule could tell time, but when it got to be five o'clock in the evening, he would stop and wouldn't move a foot until he was unhooked from whatever he was pulling. It didn't make any difference whether you were close to home or not. So Dad always had to watch the time and be close to the gate at five o'clock and no later.

That mule had another strange quirk, and that was his gate-opening ability. He could open any gate ever made. The other horses knew it too, and they all stood around and watched while he figured it out, as they knew that sooner or later he would. As soon as the gate was open, they would all step gently over the wire and follow him out.

Once Dad loaned our team to the neighbors; they probably wanted it so they could grade their road too. They were just sure that Johnny-

mule couldn't open their gates, because they had all different kinds of latches and hooks. But the mule figured them all out and let out all the stock, which made a lot of people mad. He could even figure out gates that had yards of rope tying them shut. He rolled his lips out of the way and used his teeth. He'd grab the knots and pull until he got a loose rope. He'd keep pulling until he came to the end and away he worked until the rope was on the ground. He was a handsome, black mule, a good, stout mule, and he would pull for all he was worth until five o'clock.

PROBABLY BEST OF ALL of our childhood pets was our golden collie dog. His sense of humor was even better than Honey Bunch's, and most of all he liked to ride in the special sled we made for him out of an old Atwater Kent radio case. This sled kept us entertained for hours in the winter. We'd take turns hauling it uphill for the dog. He would get in it all by himself and we'd give it a push and he'd smile all the way down the hill with his ears flapping.

He also loved the wagon. When we went to gather wood for Mom, he would ride in it until we got so much wood that he couldn't get on top of it anymore. He'd also come with us when we took the wagon to collect beer bottles to turn in for candy. When he saw a bottle, he'd jump out of the wagon and run to it and bark. Mom gave us some old red lipstick and we painted his mouth and cheeks. One of the sheep men came down from camp and saw the dog, and I can't repeat what he said. When we rode the horses, the dog wouldn't let the horse go until we helped him on so he could ride too. Sometimes he wouldn't get off when we wanted to turn the horse loose for the night, so we just let him stay on until he got ready to jump down on his own. He was our constant companion and protector who saved us from being bitten by rattlesnakes numerous times.

SO WE HAD ANIMALS instead of toys like kids have today. Of course we had a Christmas tree and we had Easter eggs too. We would decorate the Christmas tree with popcorn strings and chains of colored paper we made ourselves. We made ornaments from a kind of clay we mixed of flour, salt, and water and we painted them when they hardened. Easter eggs were quite a different story than today with all the egg paints and fancy stencils. Mom and Grandma dyed the eggs by sewing scraps of colored cloth around them and then boiling the eggs. The dye from the fabric would fade onto the eggs. We weren't allowed to watch so we didn't see them until we found them under the sagebrush where the Easter Bunny hid them.

And certainly there was no TV. We did have a radio and usually it was powered by a car battery. In later years we got a wind charger that was mounted on the roof of our house. This kept the battery charged for the radio. I can still see Dad with his ear up against the radio trying to hear the news when the battery was low. We would wish for wind to charge it again so we could listen to Fibber McGee and Molly.

MY BROTHER JOHN HAD A BICYCLE—a very old one in need of a lot of repair. He had it torn up most of the time working on it, and it never did have any brakes. He used to give my mother a terrible scare, because he would be flying down the hill and the only way he could stop would be to head sideways up a rabbit trail. Lots of times he ended up in the bushes. I always wanted to try it and one night when he had it pretty much together, he let me ride. I got out to our west gate and onto the county road and I figured that would be good because it was downhill. My brother told me that to stop I had to pedal backwards hard before I got going too fast. By the time I tried to peddle backwards, I was already out of control. I hit a dirt bank head on and landed upside down in tall sagebrush. It was a while after that before I was allowed to touch the bike.

JOHNNY WAS PRETTY HANDY at fixing that bike; he was a clever kid, all right. He was always devising games on his own and was a regular ringleader at getting us all involved. Especially when we were down in Fields for school—he could hook the entire school into his schemes. Once my dad had borrowed a flatbed trailer to haul something, and it sat around the school for a while before he took it back to its owner. John could never stand to see anything just sit that could possibly be made into something that we could have fun with, so he devised a scheme where we would all pull that trailer up the hill behind the school and then all get on it to ride down. It had a short tongue and John positioned his feet on the bars that attached the tongue to the trailer to steer it. Then he tied ropes onto the brakes for us all to pull if we needed to slow down.

We got it up and down the hill without crashing a couple of times, and then John decided that we wouldn't have to work so hard if we could use somebody's horse. One of the boys who rode his horse to school tied it to the trailer and the horse pulled it uphill. It was the funniest thing how everybody trusted John in his shenanigans when he was such a little runt until high school, but there we were like the horses that used to watch our old black mule untie the knots, waiting to see what Johnny was going to do next. It was no surprise to me that he turned out to be an engineer for NASA after going to Oregon State. I was his big sister, so I should have been reining him in or telling our folks, I guess, but I was right in there with the rest of them. Somebody's parents saw us whizzing down the hill, and Dad took the trailer back to its owner the next day.

WE HAD THE MOUNTAINS and the valleys for a playground and almost everything we did, we made into a game. There were places on the hills that were covered with shale, and those spots were real playgrounds for us. Even when we were little kids, we built miniature corrals and houses and used different sizes of rocks to stand for different animals. We devised elaborate games where we were tending to our stock, moving them out to feed and back to the corrals, putting some back in the corrals because they had eaten larkspur roots and become poisoned. We then had to give them medication. Sometimes we pretended to cure them and other times they died and we had to have a funeral and bury them. The dead grass was our hay and of course we had to build fences. Sometimes we needed a car, so that was a bigger rock. The obsidian rocks were usually our horses. We were really into this fantasy world and there was no end to what we could create, as there was an unlimited supply of raw material everywhere we looked. We had acres of hills, canyons, tall mountains with big rim-rocks, and so many things to do that our playing never had to end.

✛

WHILE WE LIVED DOWN at Fields during the bad weather, Dad used to haul hay that he bought at the Trout Creek ranches for the sheep. He hooked the iron-wheeled wagon onto the old Studebaker. The weekend entertainment for the schoolkids was to take a lunch and hitch a ride on the wagon. As the roads were just dirt and rock, it was pretty rough with those iron wheels, but what did we care. It was softer coming back, riding on top of the hay. There was a penny refund on beer bottles, so we jumped off the wagon to pick up the bottles. This was an all-day trip, so we got home about four o'clock. On school days we could hear him coming about that time. The teacher would say, "Okay, kids, hurry up and put your things away because Mr. O'Keeffe is coming!" My dad was a regular Pied Piper and all the kids loved him—we'd toss on our coats, run to meet him, climb up the ladder on the back of the wagon, and sit on the hay. By the time we got on, we were usually at the sheep-feeding ground. If there was enough snow, we hooked our sleds behind the wagon and rode on them. Dad traveled at a crawl anyway and watched out for us.

THIS OLD STUDEBAKER CAR was an all-purpose car indeed, not some kind of luxury vehicle for family outings. The roads in those days were little more than cow trails, basically dirt roads with rocks sticking up everywhere, so travel was slow and meandering. The trick to travel was to avoid high centering your car. Every year the rains would wash the dirt away from the bedrock and the road would gradually widen out in those places as everyone wound out into the sagebrush to get away from the rocks. The cars were real high and the wheels were big but that wasn't always enough to get through. We used to carry shovels to level out the road in the worst places. First we would bring smaller rocks and then we would shovel dirt into the cracks to build up a smooth area to get the car over the hump.

My job was to stand in front of the car and guide my mother across and make sure nothing was going to hit the oil pan. Sometimes she brought bridge planks to put down so we could get across some uneven spot and I had to guide her across those places, my arms flapping like a scarecrow as I directed her this way and that. It was not at all uncommon that we would high center anyway and mash in the oil pan. Mom would jack up the car and crawl under it to take off the pan. Then she would pound it out and put it back on. We always carried extra oil for just such an occasion.

THAT CAR LASTED A LONG TIME. Even going to school from the homestead in it was an adventure, as it didn't have any floorboards. First, Dad would have to work on the engine to get it to go and when he finally got the car running, there we would be in our crisply ironed clothes, riding along in a car with the rocks and road going by underneath. It was dusty, but we tried not to get our fingernails dirty, because we got stars in our health charts for clean fingernails. Whichever one of us got to sit in the front seat with Mom had to sit way back on the seat so we wouldn't fall through. Mom had to be real careful so as not to get hit on the shins when the clutch or brake pedal came up. She caught it a number of times and looked like she had a black leg. Woman in those days didn't wear long pants like they do today, and so everywhere Mom went people would say, "Guess Ben doesn't have the floorboards back in yet."

When our tires wore out, Dad would cut the inner rim out of another old tire and cover the hole. Everybody did that with their tires, as people had to make do with what they had; nothing was wasted. In fact, a wheel with only one tire looked sort of naked. The brakes weren't very good either, so we always drove downhill in low gear to be able to stop or at least head for a soft bank if needed. One day we went to Fields and the car was hot, with steam going up in a giant cloud. Dad and several other men stood out and waited for it to cool down. One fellow thought if he took off the lid it would help. He got a rag and headed for the car just as it blew the lid off and up into the air like a geyser with all the water in the radiator.

THE BIGGEST ADVENTURE was to drive to Burns, the closest town of any size, which was one hundred and thirty miles away. That's where Mom's brothers lived, and we did like to visit our cousins, even though I got carsick every time. The cousins didn't have much extra room, so we'd all have to sleep in the bed crosswise, the girls at one end and the boys at the other. Every fall Mom and Dad drove in to get big hundred-pound sacks of staples like flour, brown beans, rice, butter beans, little white beans, ham hocks, and sugar. They would also stock up on salt and coffee. All these big bags would be stored in the bedroom with Mom and Dad where it was clean and dry.

ONCE MY BROTHER AND I had to be taken to Burns to have our tonsils taken out. We were quite small then and my sister was just a baby, so the whole family went to Burns and stayed over several days for the surgery. We came home on the east side of Steens Mountain. We got a late start from Burns that day and it got dark well before we got home. We came to a draw where the bridge was out and there was no sign to show where a track went around the missing bridge. This was over by the Alvord Ranch. My brother and I were asleep in the back seat and Mom was holding the baby.

Suddenly the nose of the car went down. Dad yelled and Mom yelled at the same time. The car stopped. Fortunately, we never traveled fast on those terrible roads. The folks got out to survey the damage. The ditch wasn't very deep, three feet or so, I'd say, but we were in it with the front wheels all right, and no light to help us get out. So they hunted for rocks in the dark and built up the ditch until they could jack up the car and back out. The oil pan was partly bent in and the noise was deafening. With no light they couldn't see to take it off, so Dad just drove about five miles an hour the rest of the way to Fields. No more sleep that night, and everybody in Fields could hear us coming when we arrived in the middle of the morning. We were the noise heard around the world.

THIS WAS THE CAR OF ALL TRADES. Mom would take out the backseat and put ewes and lambs in to move from one place to another. We always had to put a lot of old gunnysacks in for them to lie on, and sometimes we would put in a fork full of hay. We took the car down by the creek bed and shoveled sand into the galvanized tubs for the cellar bins. At times we hauled some brush in back to use for wood. With Mom at the wheel it was sort of like, "Have car, will haul!" I liked it that the old car had the spare tires on either side of the front fenders and there was space for my little sister to ride there. My brother and I could straddle the headlights if the weather was nice. This was a real treat and we thought we had it all.

AT LAST THE OLD CAR was so worn out that even a genius like my dad couldn't keep it going, and he decided that we needed a new one. So with a handful of tools, chewing gum tin foil (this was a temporary fix for fuses when they blew out), extra blankets, and some food, Dad took off early one morning for Burns. The day before we had cleaned, washed, and polished the old car until it looked pretty good. Dad even had the floorboards and the mats back in. Dad took off alone and I cried. I wondered if he would make it and what would happen to all of us if he didn't. I always cried when Dad went anyplace for more than a day.

DAD MADE IT TO BURNS and stayed in the Arrow Head Hotel that night. He had parked the old Studebaker on the street by the garage. The next morning he went to the garage and bought a new car, but they said it would take a day or so to get it ready because they had to fill the oil and gas and check things out on it. While Dad was still there, a man came in looking for an old car with running gears he could use to make a hay wagon. He bought the old Studebaker for seventy-five dollars and tried to drive it away. But the old car had started for the last time, and even the garage people couldn't make the engine run. It had to be towed away to be made into a hay wagon.

DAD HAD TO BE BACK to help us feed the sheep, so he came home the next day on the stage. One of the neighbors had a son about twenty-two or twenty-three years old, and he said he would go to Burns to get the new car for us, so Dad said fine. On the day he was to arrive with the new car, we watched and waited but he didn't come. It was bedtime and still no car, so we had to go to bed. Early the next morning we got up and looked out and there it was—our new car. So we ran out and got in, only to find out that it smelled like cigarette smoke. Come to find out, that night when he was supposed to deliver our car, that young man had taken the new schoolteacher out on a date.

I WAS MAD ABOUT THE CIGARETTE smoke in our new car, but I guess it didn't matter. A new car doesn't stay new long on a ranch anyway. Ours got some pretty rough treatment from the nanny goat my folks had borrowed that year to have extra milk for the bummer lambs. That old nanny was brown and white with horns and she had lots of extra milk that we mixed with oatmeal for feed. She had the cutest little white kid with black spots and big, round, wise-looking eyes with long, curly eyelashes.

ONE MORNING WE GOT UP and the old nanny goat had blue all over her broken-off horns. At first we couldn't imagine how she had turned her horns blue, but it didn't take long to find out. There were scratch marks all over the sides of our new car. And the little goat took his turn as well. He came running full force at the car and up he went onto the hood and over the top. He slid all the way down over the trunk. The folks decided it was time to return the borrowed goats once and for all. I missed them, though, because they were awfully cute.

THE YEAR OF THE NEW CHEVROLET was my eighth-grade year at the little red schoolhouse in Fields, and that was truly one of the best years of my life. In the spring our family moved back from Fields to the ranch. Teddy and I were best of friends by then and we were both crazy about horses. She had a real pretty sorrel horse and I had my mom's big black and white pinto named Sleepy Kat. Teddy would ride up from Fields and I would ride down to meet her. Then we would go on to our house and Teddy would stay the night. The next day we would ride halfway again and I would turn around and go back to the ranch while she would go home to Fields. It was a wonderful time that spring, and sometimes we explored canyons when we went to check on the sheep. The sun was shining on the Pueblos to the south, turning them pink. We found great places to get up high where we could look over miles of open spaces and watch the cloud shadows change the shape of the mountains.

OUR LIVES WERE CHANGING SHAPE TOO, and in the typical way of teenagers, I thought of it in relation to myself instead of what this change meant to my folks. Education was important to my parents, and I needed to go to high school. The other kids were coming up in age too, so some decisions had to be made, as there was no high school at Fields. The nearest one was the boarding school at Crane where ranch kids from as far as one hundred miles away came and stayed in dormitories. This was an old school and it is still in operation today. I had visions of grandeur thinking of all the freedom I would have and the fun with so many others my age, but my folks thought the school was a little too wild. They developed a different plan that involved moving the family operation closer to Burns so we kids could go to high school there. The change took place in stages, but for me it was a traumatic experience as well as a great sadness to leave the blue foothills of the Steens. There were many times later when I wished for my old homestead home where I could climb the mountains and run free.

✤

Part II

The Green House Ranch

THE RESERVOIR BELOW OUR OLD homestead is named for my dad—O'Keeffe Springs, it's called—but otherwise the land is pretty deserted around there now, and the sagebrush we once cleared has grown back. You might see deer and antelope, but you don't see any sheep. Some of the land is still used for summer range for cattle, but you don't see too many of those either. Some twenty-five years before Dad homesteaded in the foothills of the Steens, there had been arguments between the men who ran cattle and the men who ran sheep.

It's the stuff that western movies were made of: masked riders in the night and so on. I think Dad heard about one incident almost as soon as he got off the train in Lakeview, probably because it involved an Irish herder, even though it had happened sixteen years before he got there. It wasn't the kind of story Dad told us kids, but we heard other herders talk about it when they came down the mountain with their bands and spent the night.

This happened to an Irishman who had just arrived in the States and was employed by one of the big firms, Parker and Green. He had been sent with a band of sheep a little east of Fort Rock for early summer pasture. I guess he thought that it was some sort of western joke when men with masks on came to warn him that he'd better get the sheep off that range, because he didn't do it. Well, the masked riders came back and tied up the Irish herder and blindfolded him. Some of the sheep they drove over a cliff and the rest they shot—almost two thousand of them. This kind of thing happened more than once, but it never happened on the Steens. By the time our family came along, the fighting had pretty much evened out to where a lot of the cattle and sheep men raised both kinds of livestock and the men acted civilized to each other; in fact, they became friends. They had been fighting over the same public grazing land anyway, and now it was all regulated by government permits.

Together, the cattle and sheep utilized the open range to a better extent. The sheep used the range first and ate the small tender grass and weeds while the cattle ate the tougher bunch grass. Both animals fertilized the soil so it produced a lot better. I have seen a bare piece of land used for the sheep bedding ground turn into a grassy pasture. Cow manure doesn't disintegrate as fast as the rich sheep manure, though. And cows will relieve themselves right where they are, even when they have waded into water. Sheep won't get into the water at all and won't even drink where cows have been unless forced to do so. We only had one cow on the Steens homestead, a milk cow named Lady May. Of course we had her calves too, which Dad sold every year.

Most of the arguments sheep men and cattlemen had were probably about land instead of animals. The most famous of all the land squabbles near the Steens involved a man named Peter French, who got into a fight with homesteaders who took over the lake bed land where the water had receded. It wasn't a fight between cattle and sheep; it was more about who had the rights to this government land, and the law about it was pretty confusing so both sides thought they were right. We learned about Peter French in grade school and high school both. He had wild and wooly ways and got particularly land-greedy, so somebody shot him in the end. In high school we learned both sides of the story—how the homesteader probably had a right to cut the fence and how Mr. French didn't even have a gun—but I wasn't much interested in it, to tell the truth. By then, I was interested in another man who was young and much better looking than the pictures I'd seen of Peter French.

THERE IS NO GOING BACK in time and it makes me sad to know that you never see a sheep in the area of our old homestead anymore. There are lots of reasons for that. Even in 1942 when the big change began for us, the land around the Steens was changing too. The weather seemed to be getting drier every season and the snowcapped mountains were beginning to lose their snow more and more each year. It had always been a dry and hard life in the southern Steens, and when the grass was drier than usual, the lambs didn't gain much weight, so they didn't sell for as much money. Selling the lambs in the fall provided part of the income; the rest came from selling the wool in the spring.

Another thing that made the land less hospitable for the sheep was the spread of cheatgrass. There are different theories as to exactly where cheatgrass came from and whether its introduction was accidental or deliberate, but it certainly took over the West. I don't remember any cheatgrass when I was a little girl. What I remember is that one year a man came with free seed and an offer to pay the ranchers to keep so many acres free of livestock for a year so the grass could get well established. I always thought this man was from the Taylor Grazing Office, but we blamed them for everything bad, so I may have been wrong about that. This was at a time when there was talk of overgrazing and the idea was that this was a hardy, fast-growing grass that would make great early feed for the livestock, and as it matured it would help substantiate the bunchgrass. My dad and all the other ranchers around our area signed up for the program, and my dad fenced off a part of our land. The cheatgrass got well established all right; it spread all over the country like wildfire.

Cheatgrass seeds look like short needles with backward feathers that act like little anchors. The stock would eat it when it was young, short, and green, but it matured fast, and then it was dynamite for causing trouble. The seeds got into the eyes, ears, noses, and between the hooves of the sheep, and they caused infections because they burrowed right in through the skin. For cows it was not quite as bad as it was for the sheep, as the seeds didn't stick in their hair. But they got in the wool of the sheep. They were like fish hooks, impossible to get out, so the wool was docked as dirty wool when it went to market. Once the cheatgrass got established in an area, the sheep men didn't want to graze the sheep there, because it resulted in a poor wool crop. Cheatgrass greatly increased the wildfires too, because once it dried out for the summer, it acted like kindling for any blaze that started with lightning. The whole experiment was a real disaster.

The year Dad planted the cheatgrass, the agent came back to check on how his stand was doing. Dad said, "You'd better take off your socks before you walk up on that pasture," but this fellow didn't think that was necessary so he didn't. He came back and his ankles were all bloody from all the sharp, pointed seeds that had burrowed into his socks. The agent decided right then and there that this cheatgrass was a very bad idea, but it was already a year too late.

OUR BIG CHANGE DIDN'T COME all at once; when it came, it came in stages. We lived at the homestead five miles from Fields until the fall of 1942, when I was to begin high school in Burns. Then the folks rented a little house in Burns, and we kids batched it there for the better part of a year while the folks kept the sheep at the homestead ranch. That first year I was in high school wasn't easy for us kids at all. At least we had relatives in the Burns area who would check on us and to whom we could go for help, but it was still pretty tough on my brother and me. We had the full responsibility of keeping things going, getting our meals, and getting to school clean and on time. I didn't like school at all when I first started, because the only person I knew was my cousin.

Another reason I didn't like school is because right before it started, Mom took me to the beauty salon in Burns and had a permanent put in my hair, thinking she was doing me a big favor. It was not good. That's what an old Irishman said, a harmless but sort of crazy man whom everyone in Burns called the Town Crier, when I came out of the salon just as he was walking by on the street. "Not good, Missy, not good," he said, shaking his head. My hair was in little, tight curls and I looked like a recently shorn merino sheep, blond with a reddish tinge to her wool. I cried and cried but there it was—nothing could be done about it. So when I got to school that first day, I felt very left out and ugly.

John and I shared the major chores when we stayed in the little Burns house. He did most of the outside ones, like splitting the wood and milking the cow, and I did the housework, cooking, baking our bread, and ironing our clothes with flat irons heated on the stove. My little sister Kathleen was too small to do much of anything, but she was always with us and we had to take care of things for her too. My uncles, who brought us a load of log rounds to use for the woodstove in the kitchen, gave John a wedge and an ax. My brother was only twelve years old. He was in the seventh grade, and he was small for his age, so he had a hard time splitting that wood.

Mom and Dad took turns coming to visit us from Fields, and they would bring things like food Mom had fixed or sometimes clothes. Mom would usually stay for a week or so and then go home to see how Dad was, left alone there in the mountains with the sheep where it was dangerous. He could fall, get bitten by a snake or a rabid coyote, and no one would ever know. But he wasn't the one who got hurt that year; it was Johnny. Luckily my mom was there in Burns when it happened. Aunt Inez was there too, as she was expecting a baby any time and by staying there with Mom instead of out on the ranch she could get to the hospital in a hurry.

SO THERE WE WERE in our two-room house and Johnny was outside splitting wood. He came to the door. "I cut my finger a little bit," he said.

"Let's have a look," said Mom, and then she almost fainted. Johnny's thumb was hanging on by a thread of flesh.

Aunt Inez almost fainted too, but the shock of the blood and Johnny's thumb made the baby want to come. Aunt Inez started breathing real fast and holding her stomach. "I have to go to the hospital right now," she said.

Mom grabbed her with one hand and she grabbed my brother, who was by then bleeding profusely, with the other hand and off they went to the hospital with Johnny's whole arm wrapped in a towel. At the hospital they sewed on Johnny's thumb and Aunt Inez had her baby just fine. Aunt Inez stayed at the hospital for a few days but Mom and Johnny came home and we all went back to doing what we were doing. The thumb grew back on, but it took a long time doing so, and I had to milk the cow and chop the wood until it did.

In the spring of that school year Mom boarded me out with the librarian. She took the other kids back to the Steens homestead and homeschooled them. I took the stage home when the school term ended, and when I got to Fields, the stage driver was smiling but my mother looked at me in horror. "Honey, what happened to you?" she shrieked. I didn't know what she was talking about, but the driver told Mom that the three-day measles were going around. I was entirely covered with red spots, which had broken out halfway through the trip on the stage, and I didn't even know it. I gave them to the other kids, of course, and a few days later as we were trailing the sheep across the hills to the McDade shearing corrals, Dad broke out with the measles too.

✢

THAT SUMMER WAS OUR LAST summer on the foothills of the Steens. It still makes me sad to think about it, because I had been so glad to return to the mountains and the rimrock. I looked at everything with a different eye, knowing I would never live there again. Steens Mountain seemed especially beautiful to me, and I looked hard at the wildflowers and went to all my special childhood places like the Big Seat. I even crawled back up there where Grandma had set me and that made me want to be a child again. I walked every favorite hill and went clear beyond the rimrock, looking for wild horses. It would take me a long time to get used to the flat country around Burns where there were no mountains near enough to climb.

ALREADY MY FOLKS WERE preparing for the move, and when it was time to bring the sheep down from the summer pastures, my brother and I had to go back to Burns to start school. We were alone again while Mom and Dad started to trail the whole band of sheep for a hundred and thirty miles to the Green House Ranch south of Burns, a place my folks leased from one of Mom's brothers, where we were eventually going to live.

TRAILING SHEEP IS NO EASY JOB when you have a lot of them like my dad's big band. For one thing, they go by their own time schedule and rest during the middle of the day. It takes dogs and somebody on horseback and even then things can go wrong. When they came all the way from the homestead to Burns, Mom drove the car and brought all the things that were coming on the move. Dad was on horseback with the dogs, helping him to keep track of the sheep. So for the month that it took to trail the sheep, we kids were batching it by ourselves in a little cabin in Burns that the folks had rented for us so we could go to school. We were back to the chores on our own.

WE WALKED TO SCHOOL, stopping at the grocery store on the way home to get what we could. Sometimes I just got bread and peanut butter, especially the one time Mom forgot to leave us the food ration stamps and things got pretty tight. One of our relatives would stop at the cabin once a day to see if we were doing all right, and we always said we were fine, even when we weren't. There was some pride in being able to cope with whatever came our way. We had been taught not to complain, to figure things out ourselves and to make do with what we had. Uncle Ormond, however, put us to the ultimate challenge when he showed up with the tomatoes.

UNCLE ORMOND BROUGHT US three bushels of ripe tomatoes that he bought cheap from a salesman up town who wanted to get rid of them in a hurry because they were starting to spoil. Mom and Grandma had always done most of the canning from the garden, so I didn't know quite what to do, even though I had watched and helped them many times. It was a Friday evening so I borrowed some kettles and my uncle came back with some jars. My brother and I canned all the tomatoes that weekend using the woodstove. The wood was wet and it was hard to keep the fire hot, but we did it because it had to be done. We canned sixty-three quarts and only two quarts spoiled later.

We had stayed up until midnight Sunday night finishing the tomatoes, because we knew they would be too far gone to use the next day with no refrigeration. We were so tired we could hardly sleep, even though we had school the next day. And we were jumpy, besides, because some of the soldiers who were stationed in town had gotten drunk the night before and had run their truck into the front of a lady's house along the road. This little shack my parents had rented for us was right on the

street, on a corner, in fact, and every time a car went by the lights made a glow behind the shade and this made it barely light in the room. The bedroom was tiny with two windows and only a few inches left for squeezing between the beds. That night when we were almost too tired to get to sleep, a car went by and suddenly I sat upright. There was a man standing in the doorway.

I was too scared to even scream. I reached across the little aisle between the beds and touched my brother's shoulder. He seemed to understand something was wrong, and then another car went by and Johnny saw the man in the doorway too. We froze and neither of us said a word. Then the room was dark again but we didn't move because we knew the man was still there and we were both terrified. We were trapped in that room with no way to get out and no way to get someone to come and help.

Another car went by and there was the silhouette of the man again, and he hadn't moved. Who was he and why didn't he speak? Was this a drunk soldier again who had bumbled into the wrong house for the night, or was it worse? Maybe it was the old Town Crier—he wasn't as harmless as people thought.

Of course we couldn't go to sleep knowing that man was there and not knowing what he wanted or what he might do. Each time a car went by we could see his coat and hat. Finally my brother could take it no longer and he jumped up and turned on the light. There was Dad's coat and hat on a hanger where Mom had put it on the door, and somehow it looked like a shadow when the car lights made a white light in the room. I have never been so relieved in my life.

We didn't have any furniture in this little cabin except the beds in one room, so we had filled the entire other room with the tomato jars as we finished canning. Aunt Inez stopped in the next evening to see how we were doing and all she could say was "Oh, my goodness, oh, my goodness." The next day she brought Aunt Gladys to see the sight and when she saw all the jars she just kept saying, "I can't believe your uncle Ormond would do this to you kids. I just can't believe he would do such a thing."

A few days later, when Mom drove ahead of the band of sheep she and Dad were trailing to see how we were getting along, she almost fainted when she saw the whole room filled with canned tomatoes. Everyone was just amazed to see what we had accomplished, and we felt rather proud and happy at the attention, but it had never occurred to us not to figure out how to do it. We couldn't waste the tomatoes, not out there in that desert country.

✢

I DIDN'T KNOW IT THAT DIFFICULT sophomore year at high school, but I was about to enter the most important summer of my life. By the time it was over, both my exterior and my interior landscapes would be forever changed. That had to do with Shamrock—well, Shamrock was the horse, but that was only the beginning. And it had to do with Gene, because that was the summer I met him. Before that I'd been rather afraid of boys, even though I figured they couldn't all be bad, since my brother was one. It was the girls I wanted to be friends with my first year in high school, and that was hard enough. But I'll start with the exterior landscape and the change I experienced from my Steens Mountain childhood.

I'VE ALREADY TALKED A LOT about the geography of Steens Mountain, a solitary big hunk of rock with majestic gorges and canyons. Because it's so high, the vegetation goes through several changes as you go up the mountain. No conifers like the rainy parts of Oregon, just junipers, but there are aspens and cottonwoods that turn brilliant gold in the fall.

The area between Burns and Frenchglen, the little settlement on the western foothills of the Steens, is nothing like that. Once you get out of the foothills the land is flatter than the sourdough pancakes my Dad used to make for us kids in animal shapes. Except for one big ridge you have to cross, that is, which used to be a real hair-raiser in the old Studebaker. But then you come right down to the flat land again, all the way to Burns. A long time ago the whole area was the bottom of a giant lake, and that seems perfectly plausible when you're up on the Steens, because the landscape you look out on is so very flat with some silver spots of water that quiver in the distance.

The series of lakes that are left, especially the big Malheur and Harney Lakes, expand and contract according to the rainfall and the season of the year, which makes for a specialized kind of ranching peculiar to the area around Burns. Because the lakes are so shallow and the land is so level, just an inch of rainfall above the normal amount can make the lake expand over thousands of acres. But those lakes are getting smaller and shallower all the time, even in a year of good rainfall. Homesteaders like my Mom's family moved into dry lake bed areas, built their houses on the highest land, and just put up with the fact that in the spring they would be surrounded by shallow water. They built a series of canals and dikes to regulate the flow, but in high water years these often overflowed or were breached.

MY MOM GREW UP ON my grandparents' cattle ranch in what was technically the bottom of Malheur Lake, so she was used to the changing level of the water, but the first time we went to visit her brother on his lake bed ranch and the whole road was flooded, it scared the daylights out of me. We followed two tracks with water on either side to get to the house, and the whole way I was sure we were going to drown. But I was just a little kid then; after we moved to the Green House Ranch on the old lake bed south of Burns, I got pretty used to getting wet.

The water level went down as the spring progressed, and after the cattle were taken to the higher hills north of Burns for the summer, the rancher would plant fields of grain and let the wild hay or the alfalfa grow until it was ready to cut. When the hay had been cut and stacked, the cows would be brought down to the lake for pasture again. By winter the pasture would be all eaten, the cows would eat the hay, and the surplus hay and grain would provide a nice income for the rancher. My uncles helped on my grandparents' ranch when they were at home, but when they were grown, they had hay and grain ranches of their own. So there was plowing and planting and lots of cultivating to do because they raised wheat, oats, barley, rye, and one year even peas and flax. The flax blooms a beautiful blue, so it made for a fantastic field with all the blossoms.

THE SCHOOL YEAR OF 1943–44 we kids stayed in the cabin in Burns during the week until school was out for the spring. Dad stayed with the sheep at the Green House Ranch five miles out of Burns fixing up the place, and Mom went back and forth between the family members. In early summer, right after I had finished my sophomore year in high school, we moved the sheep up to summer range, an area Dad had leased in the mountains north of Burns along the Silvies River. The war was still going on but we didn't think or talk about it much. Later I thought a lot about it because of Gene's letters or, rather, because of the lack of them at certain times. War is always a terrible thing, but it is especially terrible if you have a loved one who could be hurt or never come home. I was frightened but I couldn't show it or I would have been reprimanded, because my folks were against my feelings from the beginning.

NOW WE'RE BACK WHERE we started, with Shamrock. The ranchers all turned their horses out to forage for themselves when they weren't in use and sometimes the herds got mixed together and the breeds got mixed up too. We did not talk back then about keeping herds pure or the kind of things that they worry about today with the wild mustangs. After all, none of the horses were really native there; they had all been brought from different places by different men.

Sometime in the early 1940s a woman named Mary Kueny, who lived on the east side of the Steens on a large sheep and cattle ranch, bought a real expensive and beautiful quarter horse stallion and turned him loose on the range to see if he would produce a bigger breed of horses than the mustangs. Of course this stallion bred with all available mares on the range, which mostly belonged to the other ranchers. The mustang stallion probably protected his mares, so the quarter horse stallion didn't breed with them. One of the horses bred by Mary Kueny's stallion was Junie, a mare that belonged to my dad and had been turned loose for the season.

In those days at least once a year the government men from Taylor Grazing Service, the government agency, rounded up as many horses as they could find in order to thin out the herds. I guess this was to save the available range for the ranchers' cattle or maybe to keep the mustangs from starving to death in the winter. They would use small planes to haze them; after the planes got them together, buckaroos on the ground were herded the horses into temporary pens that the men had already set up with poles and wire. Next, they would load all the horses in trucks and take them to the agency corrals in Burns. Any horse that had a brand could be looked up in a register; the government men would contact the owners and give them a certain time to collect their horses. The rest would be shipped off to the slaughterhouse.

The year we moved from the Steens, Dad was contacted about Junie because she had Dad's brand on her. The O'Keeffe brand was a big *O* with one flattened side that had two spokes that made a *K* and then another branch coming out of the center to make an *E*. When my uncles went to pick Junie up from the Burns corral, she had two of her colts with her that Dad had branded; the big one was a beautiful bay that they thought would make a good horse for me, and the younger one ended up being my sister's horse and we called him Peanuts.

The big bay I called Shamrock and he was my lucky horse, all right. His mane and tail were curly and long and he was a truly a magnificent animal, probably part mustang like his mother Junie, but definitely an offspring of that big beautiful stallion because he was so tall. My uncles brought those horses to the Green House Ranch right before we trailed the sheep to the summer pasture, and with them was a handsome young man from Portland who was working as a hired hand for the summer. He was tall and lanky and had brown eyes like Shamrock. That was Gene.

✢

THE SUMMER OF 1944 STARTED with the sheep drive but this drive to the pasture was easy compared to what we went through when we lived above Fields. There was even a road by which we could get up to the pasture with the car to bring supplies. The lower mountains were not the same as the Steens at all, they were really just hills, but it was quite lovely as we were right along the Silvies River in an old deserted homestead we called Brown's Place.

When my friend Teddy from eighth grade and her mom came to stay with us for a while, Teddy taught us how to swim. We caught crawdads and Mom cooked them, even if there wasn't much to them, and we learned to fish. That yielded trout, perch, and suckers of all sizes and Mom cooked them too. Of course the usual wildlife was there: coyotes, antelope, deer, porcupines, and snakes. The unusual ones for us kids of the high desert were the beavers making a dam on a side creek. We sat quietly way back under the quaking aspens and watched them work, carrying sticks in their mouths to the dam and weaving them into a sort of net to keep the water in a pool.

There had been a home once at Brown's Place and part of the house remained, so we used it instead of tents. I suppose Brown was a homesteader who had given up and moved away. In those days when people left a place (and lots of people did, either to move on to something better, like my folks, or to give up and go back to where they came from), they just took what they could carry and left the rest. This was a most unusual house built right over a little creek, as if the homesteader wanted to keep cool in the summer. It had almost fallen in by the time we got there, but there was one room downstairs and one room upstairs that were still solid, with a screen porch along the side. We girls had the upstairs room, Mom and Dad had the downstairs room, and when Teddy and her mom came to visit, they slept on the screen porch. My brother John had his bedroom in a little three-sided shed. He made a bunk bed there and slept on top because he didn't want any of the wildlife crawling into bed with him.

ONE MORNING WE WOKE UP and looked out into the green meadow. Sometime in the night a big bay horse had arrived, obviously looking for company. He was tame and had been ridden before, but he was blind in one eye. By asking around we found out that he had been abandoned and it was okay to keep him, so we did. We named him Cyclops because of his single eye, and we even took him back to the Green House Ranch at the end of the summer. He lived for many years and we all loved him.

AT FIRST THAT SUMMER I was too busy exploring the area, watching the sheep, and having a good time with Teddy to think too much about Gene. But he must have been thinking of me because he spent an awfully lot of time breaking my horse to ride. While I was up in the mountains with the sheep and those three horses were down at the Green House Ranch, my uncles took it upon themselves to look out for my future romantic interests. They told Gene they thought he should gentle my horse for me, so he got the three horses into a corral and he started working with Shamrock. Gene loved horses almost as much as I did, and he surely enjoyed doing this in the evenings after working all day for my uncles. He and another young man named Red Inman were sleeping at the ranch house that summer while all of our family was up at the sheep camp in the hills.

Breaking a horse isn't rodeo riding; it's gaining the animal's trust and showing it that you're not going to hurt it, and Gene was the right kind of person for that. Junie and her two colts probably thought they had gone to horse heaven anyway to come down to the ranch and have all that green grass just for the taking instead of having to spend their days scrounging through the brush for a mouthful of decent food.

The first thing to do when you break a horse is to get the horse used to you, and you do that by speaking quietly and spending time with it in the corral. Gene must have done that in the evenings, because he was working crew with my uncles during the day, bucking hay and harvesting grain, and sometimes they worked pretty long hours.

After the horse is used to you and you can walk around it without it watching you all the time, you slip a rope around its neck and a loop around its nose. It helps to have a handful of grain that the horse can't resist, and then you need to keep talking gently and give it some time to adjust to the feel of the rope before you teach it to lead. After the horse is used to the rope, you start pulling gently and when it follows you, pet it some more and reward the horse with a little more grain. A horse will need some time to recognize that the pull has rewards because it's more natural to jerk against the pull.

Now you need a gunnysack, a big, old, brown gunnysack, the kind you have plenty of on a ranch but you hardly ever see today. You take that sack and you rub it all over the horse so it associates the sack with a feel-good kind of situation, like being stroked. Then you start flipping it around the horse, under its belly, over its back, and even up around its ears and face. This is in preparation for the saddle blanket and saddle, of course, and when the horse pretty much ignores the sack it's time for the real thing. Put the saddle blanket on the horse and lead it around with the blanket on its back. Don't hurry this step.

The saddle is more of a tricky business for the horse and takes a few weeks. You get the saddle on and then let the horse loose in the corral for a half a day, then a whole day after that. Pretty soon it will not react negatively to the weight on its back, though each horse is different. If you have taken enough time and if you have already won the horse's trust, this will go smoothly and the horse won't fight the saddle. The wilder ones often spend quite a bit of time bucking or even rolling to get the saddle off, but if they do, you haven't done your work right. But Gene had done his work right and when it was time to actually get on the horse, Shamrock didn't even buck. Gene had won the horse's trust. After that, he won mine.

✢

ONCE GENE HAD SHAMROCK basically gentled, it was my turn, so the horse needed to be brought up on the Silvies River for me to finish. The uncles and Gene loaded Junie, Shamrock, and Peanuts on the flatbed truck with the wooden sides and started up the rocky road to Brown's Place. That's when they almost lost my horse in the river.

SIDE ROADS LIKE THE ONE to Brown's Place were basically the responsibility of the people who used them, bridges and all, and passage was never a sure thing from one year to the next. To get to our sheep camp and corrals, the Silvies River had to be crossed, and the bridge we used to do that was so rickety that we often parked our car on the other side and carried everything across on foot. The day they came up with Shamrock, however, we had our car across the bridge beside the old house and were eating a late dinner after coming in with the sheep. That's when we heard quite the commotion and all went tearing out of the house.

The bridge had broken. There sat the flatbed truck with its back wheels hanging through the floor of the bridge where it had just collapsed under the weight of three horses, and those three horses were mighty scared, rearing and snorting, and the whole remaining bridge floor was shaking. It was ready to dump—bridge, truck, and all—sideways into the river. It wasn't that the river was deep; in fact, it was at its summer low, but it was a ten-foot drop to the water, and if that truck went in upside down, spilling horses and men, legs could be broken or worse, if horses or men got trapped under the truck.

What had been meant to be a simple horse delivery turned into quite an adventure, and a dangerous one at that. First the men had to get out of the truck, which was no mean operation, as they had only a few inches on the sides to work with. Then they had to extricate the three terrified horses and get them off the remaining shaky boards of the bridge. Dad waded the river to be on the other side to take the horses. It was terrible to watch as the horses came out of the truck because they could have broken through the strained boards or hurled sideways into the river, but we couldn't look away.

Shamrock reared and screamed in terror as the bridge swayed some more, but Gene and Dad got him off the bridge before any more boards collapsed, and the other horses followed. We had quite a time leading the horses through the river and into the corrals, and it took unexpected days of work to get that bridge fixed up and the truck pulled out of the floorboards. There is absolutely nothing like a good scare to bring your feelings into sharp focus. When Gene led Shamrock off the bridge, I could have kissed him right there, but of course I didn't.

So for most of the remaining summer I rode Shamrock and he truly became my horse. Gene came up now when he could get away and helped me work Shamrock and sharpen his skills. We got Junie back in shape too, and we even started on Peanuts for my sister. My friend Teddy was there for part of the time and whenever we could leave the sheep, we went riding together. I don't know how many miles we rode, but it turned into a beautiful summer.

Sometimes the uncles came up for a visit and they would always bring Gene, so Teddy and I and Gene would go for a ride. Teddy rode Junie and Gene rode behind me on Shamrock. I guess you could say we were getting close. Shamrock loved to jump and sometimes we even let him do that over fallen logs. I wasn't supposed to jump him; in fact, I had been specifically warned against it because the folks were afraid he'd fall on me and break my leg.

ONCE WHEN I WAS RIDING SHAMROCK, I got him jumping over all the downed hay that lay in windrows in long slabs waiting to be raked. That wasn't so smart because newly cut hay is very slick when it lays in rows that way, and Shamrock slipped on it and came down on his side. He rolled over on me but I grabbed the saddle horn, pushed as hard as I could, and managed to get my leg out from under him. I got up and he got up too. He whinnied softly and nuzzled me all over to make sure I was all right, but I wasn't, really. I was pretty bruised up, but luckily in places it didn't show. I didn't dare even complain to the folks because I'd have to explain how it happened. I should have learned my lesson but I have to admit that I kept on jumping him anyway when I was out of my parents' sight. I just didn't let him jump on the slippery hay.

I WAS SO EXCITED TO HAVE my own beautiful horse, a magnificent horse that regarded me as the only human in his life. After that summer Shamrock wouldn't come to anyone but me, and he would try to buck others off who wanted to ride him, even my dad. He would answer when I called him and I could ride him with just a rope on the halter, guiding him with my knees. That doesn't happen with all horses, but once it does, you have a one-man horse; it's almost like falling in love. For the horse, I mean.

THIS SEEMED LIKE THE ENDLESS summer because so many things happened and there was so much moving from place to place: the Brown Place; the Korten Place east of Burns, where my mother and sister stayed with the sheep while the haying was going on at Green House Ranch; the Varien Place, which was next to where my Uncle Ormond lived. That was where Teddy and I spent hours riding on the tractor with Gene when he was disking for the night crew. All these places had been homesteaded by families and later acquired by my uncles as they built up their agricultural operation. Each piece of land still held the former owners' names like some sort of living blend between geography and genealogy that lingered for a generation at least before the ghosts went away.

UNCLE ORMOND HAD GRADUATED from Oregon State—it was called Oregon Agricultural College then—and he was willing to try experimental methods, so my uncles were always one step ahead of the game in lake bed grain operations. They even invented a variation of a drill for planting so they could operate right on the edge of the retreating waterline each spring and tunnel the seeds into the moist soil. They had to have special wide treads on the tractor wheels, which they made with boards, to keep the tractor from sinking in the mud. Their enterprise was so large by the time my parents joined the family team that financially it turned out to be beneficial to all. During harvest they ran both a day crew and a night crew to finish the crops in a timely fashion and all of us worked together.

AFTER THE GRAIN FIELDS WERE harvested, Dad bought the use of the grain pasture from the uncles for the lambs. Sheep get a lot of forage that way because they eat the stubble and any grain that gets left on the ground. That, along with the good food in the hills and more meadow pasture in the fall before shipping, made for much fatter lambs and a better income for our family. And change was coming for open range stockmen anyway, with the BLM and the fences. It was a good move in lots of ways; the folks made this change for us to go to high school, for a greener place to live, and for a better lifestyle for the family. But I didn't quite understand what it meant to my dad to give up on the homestead, the place that was soaked with the sweat of his youth. And the move didn't mean that any of us, especially Dad and me, ever forgot the Steens.

Toward the end of the summer my folks leased sheep pasture from my uncles at a ranch east of Burns that they called the Korten Place. When it was haying time, Mom and Kathleen stayed there with the sheep and Dad, John, Teddy, and I all went back to the Green House Ranch to help with putting up the hay. Teddy's mother had gone to relatives in San Francisco, but Teddy stayed, and she and I cooked for everyone, which included Dad; Uncle Dick, who ran the haying operation; my brother John; the other cousins; and a few hired hands. At first Gene was on the hay crew too, but later he was over driving a cat—the D-4—disking on the night shift at the Varien Place. They always put him on the biggest machinery because he was turning into a fantastic mechanic. It wasn't just horses Gene could handle; he could make even the most stubborn tractor run.

TEDDY AND I GOT UP AT FIVE every morning and so did Dad. We had to get the woodstove going and breakfast ready for the crew so they could be in the field by six. That part of the summer was especially exciting as there were several of us young people together, and Teddy and I were the only girls. Sometimes all the guys went to town without us and came home late, so we started playing pranks on them when they did. Once we put a bucket of water on a little shelf over the kitchen door and tied a string to the bail. The other end of the string we tied to the door, so the bucket tipped down and soaked them as they came in the door that night. We got a couple of the boys good, but that joke turned out to be not so funny when they got hit with the bucket. Those old heavy galvanized pails packed a real punch and someone could have been seriously hurt.

Teddy and I had a fantastic time cooking together even though it was terribly hot that summer and we had to keep the wood fire going all the time. What's a little discomfort when you have a friend to share your dreams with and when you're young and just on the cusp of falling in love? Not that there was much time for Gene and me to get to know each other; every day, Teddy and I had to get the dishes all done, the kitchen cleaned, and then get things partly ready for breakfast the next morning. But the evenings were long, and often we two rode the horses to the grove of willows or all of us rode the five miles to the natural pool that was lined with wood and fed by the hot springs near Burns. This was a great swimming hole and it was the official swimming pool for Burns. There were trees around it and green grass with lights that stayed on all night. It was beautiful and stayed open for years.

The Green House Ranch had an old two-story house. The hired help slept upstairs with their bedrolls, and Teddy and I had the bedroom downstairs. Dad slept on the davenport in the living room and he was pretty watchful so not much romance went on. Some romance went on anyway, though, for Gene and I had figured out that we could sneak a quick kiss if we both rode our horses behind the willow stand in the lower field. Teddy knew what was happening but she didn't tell, like my sister later did.

TEDDY AND I HAD ONE MORE adventure with Gene before Teddy left to join her mother. After the haying was done and the crew dispersed, we had a few days to play, so we rode our horses to see Gene, who by that time was working several miles away. We went to see him in the guise of visiting family. It was an all-day ride. We stopped for lunch with Aunt Inez and Uncle Henry and then rode on to Rye Grass, where Aunt Gladys and Uncle Ormond had Gene driving a cat and disking on the night shift. Teddy and I rode on the cat with Gene for several hours before we went back to Uncle Ormond's house and went to bed.

The night that we rode with Gene on the cat was an important moonlit night in my life. I'd always liked being outside in the moonlight. In the sheep camp I'd sit out there with Dad at night and he would recite his poetry or start a story. Or maybe we'd just sit there without talking at all, watching the fires of herders on the side of the mountain grow dim and listening to the singing of distant coyotes and the soft murmur of sleepy sheep.

Just riding along at night on a tractor with someone who had already caught your eye probably wouldn't seem very romantic—or the place to realize that you were in love—to kids now. Gene and I weren't even alone, so obviously nothing big happened. But I think kids have it backwards today with all this quick and easy sex. To my mind that's not where love starts at all. It starts slowly by doing things together that you already love: riding horses, being outside in the moonlight—even if you're on a tractor. Or maybe especially if you're outside on a tractor; then you know what kind of work you could do together if your lives ended up joined.

I lay there unable to sleep that night at Uncle Ormond's house because Gene had told us he would be leaving. He had lied about his age and signed up with the Merchant Marines. The war was still going on and his two brothers were already over there fighting and Gene felt he should go too, so in October when the harvest was over, he would report for duty. Always before the war had seemed far away and impersonal; no one I knew or loved was affected directly by it, so it was easy to think it wasn't really happening at all. I wanted to cry like I'd cried when the army man wanted to buy Black Beauty. Dad had refused to sell him for three hundred dollars and gave him to Billy instead. If it was worth giving up three hundred dollars to save the life of a beautiful horse, how much would it be worth giving up to save the life of a beautiful man—a beautiful man with whom I'd just fallen in love?

✦

JUST AT THE TIME ALL THIS happened, Mom and my little sister Kathleen came back to the Green House Ranch with the sheep, and Teddy left to join her mother in San Francisco. Gene hadn't left yet for the Merchant Marines, but we both felt the impending separation looming before us. He took every chance he could to come and see me, and of course my folks figured out quickly what was happening. Dad had probably realized it during the summer but he didn't say anything, no doubt thinking it was just young love and would pass quickly once the summer was done. Or maybe he just thought that with Teddy almost always with us not much could happen anyway.

OUR FOLKS HAD ALWAYS BEEN strict with us, especially with my brother and me. Strict and careful too, because they didn't want us to turn into lazy, uncouth hooligans just because we lived clear out in the wild. The hunters from Salem who came to the Steens in the fall would bring us kids big stacks of comics and we would be so excited to read them. But Mom and Dad would sit down and weed them out to make sure we weren't going to be exposed to what they considered trash, and we were left with a spindly pile. So we'd been taught our manners, all right, and we knew we were expected to behave properly, but we were all entering uncharted territory now.

Even before that summer I'd had lectures from Mom about the danger of being with boys. In fact, from the way Mom talked about them before I started high school, you'd think there was one behind every sagebrush bush waiting to ravish me as I went by. This was quite baffling to me as all the boys I knew at the time were perfectly nice and no more interested in me than I was in them. But after Mom and Kathleen came back to the Green House Ranch, the lectures took on a more urgent tone. It started with the strangest incident, which we never spoke of later to each other.

I CAN'T IMAGINE THAT MOM would have told little Kathleen, who was not even twelve, to keep an eye on me, but maybe she did, because Kathleen tagged along incessantly no matter what I was doing. When Gene managed to come over, we would saddle up the horses and there my little sister would be right behind us, saddling up Peanuts as if she'd been asked to come along. Which she hadn't. After a couple of times of that nuisance, I said to her, "Kathleen, you can't come this time."

"Why not?" she shot back just as snotty as any eleven-year-old girl can, especially if she is talking to her older sister.

"You just can't, that's why," I said. I didn't owe my little sister any explanation.

"You're going to play kissy-face with Gene, I know it," she snapped. "And if you don't let me come, I'm going to tell Mom."

Well, we left her in the dust of the corral and galloped off across the field. She finished saddling Peanuts and then she came after us for a while but our horses had longer legs so soon she gave up. And she went back and told Mom, all right. I don't know what all she said, but when Gene and I peeked out from behind the willows, we could see them up on the roof. Both of them. Not just my little sister, but my mother was up there too. My mom had taken the ladder and the binoculars and climbed up on the roof to see where we were going. I couldn't believe it and I instantly felt a wave of something—shame, I guess. They couldn't see us, though. We were behind the willows and could have done absolutely anything we pleased without them knowing, but we could see them. Gene and I laughed but it wasn't a laughing matter, really.

Whatever was my mother thinking? This wasn't like her at all. For all the hard work she did and the isolation of our living conditions on the Steens, my mother had a certain grace and sophistication about her all the time. She was educated and intelligent and the herders my dad hired always treated her respectfully, almost as if she were royalty. For all her handiness with the switch when we were naughty, we kids knew she was an extraordinary woman and we were lucky to have her for a mom. But this was too much and it still embarrasses me to this day.

I think it embarrassed her too, because she didn't refer to it directly when we came back and the ladder was nowhere in sight. But I got the lecture of all lectures that night—about how girls get pregnant and what a disgrace it would be to all of us, how embarrassed I would be the rest of my life, and how there was no one to take care of raising a baby. At first I was stunned that she was talking that way, but when I went to bed later, I found myself angry. She was giving me no credit—my mother, who had given me credit for being able to handle any situation I encountered with the sheep: coyotes, rattlesnakes, the blind staggers, to name a few. And now she was giving me absolutely no credit for having any sense at all.

I understood this a little better after I had a daughter of my own, but I still find it amazing that my parents were so hostile to Gene— Gene, whom everyone else seemed to adore because he was such a conscientious, hard worker, always on time, giving any job his all, and quick to adapt and handle any situation even with the complicated new machinery that sometimes my uncles didn't understand themselves. How could anyone not like Gene, who had a ready smile for everyone, who helped with every chore no matter how trivial, who was almost as gentle as Steens Mountain Ben himself?

I know my parents were afraid of me short-circuiting my life without a thought to my own future because I was madly in love. That's because they thought I was confusing sex with love—but they were the ones who were wrong. I knew more than they thought I knew. I wasn't the one confusing sex with love; they were the ones confusing love with sex.

You don't grow up on a ranch and not figure out the facts of life. Now, we did swallow the story about the stork when we were little. In fact, the first time Johnny and I saw a sandhill crane at a little lake on the mountain (an unusual sight at our elevation, although cranes were common on the flooded fields by Burns), we went tearing back to the house to see if a baby had arrived, because we were sure we had seen a stork. Dad laughed until he had to sit down with tears running down his face.

But a situation of mistrust between parents and their kids about sex is no laughing matter at all. I knew all about sex. We had dogs, cats, goats; I knew where baby lambs came from and why the cow had to be taken down the mountain to a bull when she was in season. And I knew very well that sex did not necessarily have anything to do with love. It was a natural urge, which the animals weren't very discreet about, and there certainly were natural consequences to look out for. Why didn't they give me credit for knowing that?

ONE NIGHT SHORTLY BEFORE he left for the service, Gene borrowed Uncle Dick's car and took me to a show in Burns. I didn't really ask if I could go; it didn't occur to me that I needed permission, I guess, when I had always run free in the mountains and had been given so much responsibility at such a young age. I just said I was going and there was this long silence, so I knew things had changed. There wasn't a happy welcome for Gene that night, but we ignored it and away we went.

We went to the show and I didn't get home until about eleven. Mostly Gene and I talked that night because the time was getting close for him to leave and we were both nervous about it. Gene tried to explain to me how he felt honor-bound as a young man to face the same situation as his brothers faced, to not shirk his duty to his country, to be the kind of man I might someday want to marry. I tried to understand that feeling, but I kept thinking about Black Beauty, and I told Gene that story.

MY EYES MUST HAVE BEEN puffy when I came down for breakfast in the morning, and Mom probably thought I was crying about something else. That's the only way I can understand her remark.

"Aren't you ashamed of yourself?" she said.

"Why?" I asked. I really didn't know what she meant.

"For doing what you did last night."

Again, I was stunned, and my face felt red as I understood what she was really asking. "I'm not ashamed," I said, the tears starting up again. I felt like I had cried all night because Gene was going to the war. "We just went to the show and I am not ashamed of anything I did."

She just looked at me with her mouth set firmly and I knew she didn't believe me.

Before I admit what I said next, you have to understand that I had never talked back to my mother in my life. I loved my parents and I didn't understand at all why she and Dad were so against Gene. Most of all I didn't understand why they didn't have any faith in my judgment. They were hurting me and it made me want to hurt them back.

"Mom," I said. "Are you judging me by what you and Dad did?"

That was the end of that conversation.

✢

SO GENE WENT OFF TO WAR in the fall of 1944 and I went back to high school. I hadn't been a super academic star at school those first couple of years because I had so many chores to keep up and I didn't have a lot of time for homework. To be honest, high school was boring. It seemed to be mostly busywork that I felt was a waste of time, and the lessons were too repetitive. Luckily, studies came easy for me, so I'd basically kept up with things, even that first year when we kids were mostly by ourselves. I would get the dinner, wash the dishes while the other kids did their homework, and after that I would get them off to bed. Then I would sit down in the quiet of the evening with the gas lantern or the coal oil light and often I would wake up in the wee hours of the morning with my head on the book, cold and with my homework still not done.

One day when I was sent to the principal's office for not having finished my work, I was given an assignment to write five hundred words about why I hadn't completed it. I wrote nearly ten pages and after that the teacher and I got along much better. But I was never as happy at high school as I'd been in the one-room school at Fields. At Fields we had to be creative about everything and teach each other and there wasn't any reason to be mean to other kids. Even as an older child I was not embarrassed to take my fantasy drawings to the teacher, who encouraged me to write about them. I made them into stout little books that I figured out all myself and the teacher thought I was quite smart. And in that time homework was a family affair.

AT FIELDS WE HAD ALL BEEN so eager for companionship that there was little fighting among ourselves. We all played together at games and any competitions would be friendly or just girls against boys. And of course we were all so dirt poor that there was no social stratification. It was different at Burns and those who were a little less poor than the rest of us sometimes let us know about it. "You'd wear the same outfit to every dogfight," one of those girls said to me once. I had three dresses that I kept clean and ironed and rotated in a sequence and it hadn't once occurred to me that I needed more. That was the first time I realized that we qualified as poor. But at least I had a little circle of friends who were probably as poor as I was.

IT SHOULD HAVE BEEN EASIER to get to high school with a school bus making the route instead of the old Studebaker, but somehow we were always in trouble with the principal for being late. In fact, we were late so many times that he kept a special book for our excuses. "Well, which was it this time?" he would say. "High water, a runaway horse, or you got behind a bunch of cattle being driven somewhere and couldn't get through the road?" I'm sure we were a legend in the teachers' lunchroom.

It isn't like the school bus actually came to our house. We rode our horses down our extremely long lane and left them in a corral by an old abandoned house. When we got to the old house, we took off the saddles and tied the horses to the manger Dad had built there and fed them hay for the day. Then we changed out of our jeans, put on our school clothes, and walked about a quarter of a mile to the blacktop highway to catch the bus. If we were late we had to go home, but sometimes if the bus driver saw us he would wait as we ran down the rest of the lane. I think he felt sorry for us, to tell the truth, and sometimes when we got off the bus at the end of the day he would slip us each a candy bar as we left.

Riding the bus worked well when everything was dry and the fields weren't flooded over the lane. But in the spring of the year, when the water was at its highest, it was another story. When the water got to a certain level, the bridges along the lane that were in place over the flooded canals would float and wobble when the horses stepped on them. Shamrock and Cyclops handled this fine, but Peanuts had to be literally towed across with a rope on my saddle horn and with Johnny switching him from behind.

Sometimes the water got so deep that the horses had to swim. When that happened, we kids would put our school clothes in a gunnysack and if we didn't hold the sack high enough, we were stuck with wet clothes all day. When we got to the old house, we had no choice but to put on these wet clothes and hope they dried fast. It was embarrassing to me and there were times that I wore my coat all day to cover up a wet outfit.

The worst time was once when I was carrying a navy blue wool skirt in the gunnysack and it got completely soaked. The water didn't show, but it was early in the spring and I was awfully cold. I stood by the register and tried to warm up, but the steam started to rise from my skirt and the teacher came running over yelling, "Fire!" so everyone turned around and looked at me. My face got extremely hot and I wanted to die on the spot, but I just went to my desk and sat down without meeting anyone's eyes. I was not exactly what you would call high on the social register in high school, but by that junior year I didn't care at all. I was waiting for letters from Gene.

AS SOON AS GENE LEFT for the service, he started writing me letters, and I replied to every single one. At first the folks didn't say anything; they surely figured he would be gone long enough for things to cool down and I would be off in college by the time he came back from the war. They talked to me about that and of course I said I would go to college if they wanted me to. It seemed so important to them and I was anxious to please them, even though there was a strange wall between us now, even between Dad and me—and we had always been such easy pals. The only time it felt natural anymore was when we were out working with the sheep.

Maybe if I had understood what Dad was going through as he had to reconsider his life with the sheep, we wouldn't have gotten into such a tangle. Dad was smart enough to see the big picture, and the open range was more and more enclosed. Although there were still unfenced pastures up high, which could be leased for summer grazing, he could no longer find men whom he could trust to help him keep herd on the sheep. I didn't fully comprehend his feelings about this until I read some of his poetry later. He always tried to cloak his feelings in satire or humor, but when I read his words closely the sadness showed.

We were at the very end of an era, and it's hard to see that when you're living it. You keep thinking you can make it the way it used to be when you were happy. Dad wanted to stay in sheep ranching, but there were decisions to be made, and providing for the educational future of his kids was one of them. He bought some cattle, but I don't think he ever had quite the same feeling for them as he did for the sheep. He made more money with them, though, and they were easier to take care of because they didn't have to be watched so closely. But when you're a teenager it isn't your parents' problems that are most important in your mind; it's your own. And the most important thing in my mind was that the letters had stopped coming from Gene.

MY FIRST THOUGHT WAS that somehow Gene had been killed in the war. He was initially sent to Catalina Island for two-and-a-half months for boot camp training and after that he traveled all over, mostly to the South Pacific, hauling fuel to the troops wherever they needed it. He worked in the boiler room, keeping up the steam for the ship's power, so it wasn't like he was getting shot at every day, but it was a dangerous job as safety standards for the crew weren't as high on the list as they should have been. He wrote a lot of letters and even though censors marked out some of the words, most of them came through. Enough anyway that Mom started complaining about it. I should have known that my parents were going to apply some censorship of their own.

I started going to the post office from school during the noon hour to see if there was mail for me. At first there were letters almost every day, but after a few more weeks, there weren't any letters at all. I didn't know it, but Mom had talked to the postmaster and asked him to keep all of our mail back and not give any out to anyone, even me. I was humiliated. But Gene must have figured something was happening; he wrote to one of my friends and we devised a system where he would address the letters to her and put only his numbers on the return address to indicate it was for me. Of course this was exciting to high school girls, but it only furthered the distrust between my parents and me.

SO THERE I WAS, someone who had never talked back to her parents in her life, doing all sorts of things behind their backs. That is a slippery slope and once your mom and dad have put you in the position to sneak around, they have already lost the game. Mom and Dad didn't have a chance, really, because even the other relatives sided against them, all the uncles and Grandma too, who lived in a small house in Burns with Uncle Dick. They all thought Mom and Dad were too strict with me. They knew Gene well from the quality of his work, and they knew he would have a perfectly good financial future with his understanding of the machinery that was displacing all the horses.

Grandma may have been feeling her own regrets over her arguments with my mother at this same stage of the game. She never talked about it, but Mom had told me once that Grandma hadn't wanted her to marry Dad because he was Irish. Lots of people didn't like the Irish in those days. When he got off the ship at Ellis Island, Dad saw signs on businesses that said, "No Irish may apply." And Grandma may have objected because of the sheep. Mom's people raised crops and cattle and had popular misconceptions about sheep: that they ruined the pasture by eating all the grass that cattle needed (sheep eat tender grass and weeds and cows eat bunch grass) and that sheep spread weed seeds that get caught in their wool. Anyone who has been around sheep knows that once a seed gets in wool it is there to stay.

Grandma got over those things and she learned to love my dad too. But her initial opposition proves that the tension our once close family was going through was not peculiar to my situation or even to the dreams the folks had for my education. I was the eldest child and I guess my parents were practicing parenting teenagers for the first time. With my younger brother and sister, they weren't nearly so strict, but they sure made mistakes with me.

✢

IN THE MEANTIME the ranching operations went on and I worked hard as I always had and none of us mentioned the obvious problem between us. I had gone totally underground with my feelings around my parents. I had seen Gene after he went into the service but the folks didn't know about it. He had come home on leave right before he was shipped out. We met at my Grandma's house and we both stayed there with Grandma and Uncle Dick. I often stayed overnight with Grandma then and the folks thought it was nice that we were so close. I'd always loved Grandma and when we were together we'd talk about the Steens. "Remember the Big Seat?" she would ask me every time and she was pleased that I not only remembered it but that I thought of it with love. And I wasn't lying when I said I wanted to spend time with her; she seemed to understand me now far more than my own mother did.

Gene and I had time alone yet we weren't alone at all, so everything was perfectly proper. That was a quiet, deep time in our relationship and neither of us doubted any more that it would continue. I felt, though, when I went back with Mom and Dad, that I was leading this strange double life that I didn't feel guilty about anymore at all. It was just an inevitable fact by then and we were all going through the motions as if things were the same as they'd been when I was still a child.

BUT I DID MY PART on the ranch as I always had. Mom and I traded off with the summer pasture for the sheep. I guess I was the happiest there, even when I was there alone, because I could think my own thoughts without interruption. When you are young and so in love, what difference does it make what goes on around you? But when it was my turn back on the ranch with the haying operation, there was no time for dreams about the future. By this time we worked with a combination of horses and machinery but it still took all hands on deck to get it done when the hay was ready. There was even a special vocabulary for the operation that only those who have been there can really picture now in their minds: setting the net, driving the bucks, the pull-up tractor, the pull-back horse, the mower, the rake, the slide. We all had to know how to operate everything, and Mom was one of the best. We worked together and neither of us mentioned Gene.

I GOT TO SEE GENE ONLY one other time when I was still in high school, and it was a total surprise. Gene and two of his buddies from Portland were based in Los Angeles and they had a short leave between ship assignments to the South Pacific. They bought a car between them and he convinced his buddies to drive over to Burns. Gene came right into the high school to see me and I almost died of shock. There he was, handsome and tall in his uniform, and he grabbed both my hands and kissed me right there in the hallway. The whole visit was just for a few minutes; I had to go to class and if I had skipped out, the principal would have called my parents.

When I walked into class late, I knew my face was burning red but this time I wasn't ashamed the way I had been when I came to school with the wet blue skirt. I didn't care at all that every girl was staring at me, because this time all the other girls were absolutely open-mouthed with undisguised envy, and I loved it.

THE SPRING OF 1946 I graduated from high school and by that fall I was in Monmouth at the Oregon College of Education. Most of our family has ended up at Oregon State throughout the years, but Mom and Dad had in mind for me to be trained as a teacher. That was all right with me. For me college meant freedom and the chance to get letters from Gene. I don't know what Mom and Dad thought—maybe they thought they had won the war because there were no letters that came for me at home and I never mentioned him at all.

EXCEPT FOR THE FREEDOM, I wasn't much happier in college classes than I'd been in high school. They were so regimented and boring and once you have learned how to teach yourself whatever you need or want to know in the great outdoors, it's hard to listen to someone who thinks it all has to be done their way and done inside to boot. I had thought of majoring in art because I enjoyed drawing so much. But when I turned in an assignment on fantasy that had some of the gargoyle kind of figures that were leftover in my mind from the Ascripfa dreamland, I got back a nasty comment in red. "Never turn in anything like this again," it said. I was shocked and hurt and have no idea why it so upset the teacher.

I TOOK ANOTHER ELECTIVE that was more craft-oriented; the object was to make a book with an attractive hard cover and blank pages. There were specific instructions on how to construct the binding so it wouldn't crack. I had been making books since my leftover ballot days, and I had invented my own way to construct the binding, so I used that. When I went in for my project review, the teacher was furious because I hadn't followed the directions exactly. "Your binding will break," said the teacher, a strange, skinny lady who narrowed her eyes whenever she talked to you. This time I decided not to take it lying down.

"It will not," I shot back. "Let me show you." I took the book from her and I showed her how the binding would actually be more protected the way I had constructed my book. She didn't argue; in fact, she didn't say anything at all, but she must have examined my book later and realized I was right because somewhere along the line my failing grade was changed to an A+.

THE FUNNY THING WAS, I was awfully homesick sometimes at college. Only I wasn't quite sure what to be homesick for. I'd never really felt the same about living at the Green House Ranch as I'd felt about the homestead. And now things were so unhappy there with my parents that it felt even less like home. I anxiously awaited Gene's letters and I felt that my future would be with him but in the short run I was lonely and felt rather adrift. I was again between worlds and when I dreamed at night, it was always of the Steens.

✢

WHEN GENE CAME HOME from the service early in 1947, the first thing he did was come to college and visit me. I can't even tell you how glad we were to see each other, and I think we both knew then that we were in this for life. He came down several times to see me and all was fine until I went home for the summer.

After Gene's first visit to Green House Ranch, my mom and dad sat down with me and tried to talk. They said they didn't want me to see Gene any more at all. I heard that much with a clear mind. I was way too young, my dad said, to be so serious about someone, and young marriages like that just didn't have a good chance of lasting for life. He wanted me to finish college, to make sure that all avenues were open to me in the future, because the world was changing fast.

His was a rational approach and I had intended to finish college no matter how much I was in love with Gene. I would probably have promised them that if Mom had just kept quiet. But she didn't. "We thought you would go to college and find a lawyer or doctor to marry," she said.

That pushed me over the edge. Here was my mother—my mother who had gone to college yet married a man with only a few sheep to his name because she loved him, and she was telling me to marry someone with more financial potential than she saw in Gene. She had married Dad over her own mother's objections since Grandma had been nervous that Ben O'Keeffe was a foreigner and might not get full citizens' rights. Mom and this penniless immigrant had carved their living out of the mountain, the rugged Steens, and a beautiful living it had been, doing what they both loved, meeting every challenge together, from rabid coyotes to losing the sheep to the bank. And Mom loved that man still. Didn't she think that I wanted the chance to do the same?

How could she possibly think I would want to marry someone for his money—especially someone who was likely to live in a city and be a doctor or a lawyer? I was an outside girl, a child of Steens Mountain; she had told me herself that I was the hardiest baby that ever lived. Money meant little to me, because they had taught me that it had nothing to do with happiness. They had taught me that what you needed for a meaningful life and a lasting marriage was freedom on the mountain, the beauty of nature, and the courage to meet challenges together.

But I didn't say any of that—I was only nineteen, and that's too young to have the right answers in arguments with your parents, even if you feel the right answers inside, because neither of you have let go of the old relationship.

"OH!" I SAID ANGRILY. "I thought you sent me to college to get an education; I didn't know you were throwing away money hoping I would catch a man." My words were sharp-edged and I wanted them to hurt. "Well, I didn't meet any doctor or lawyer I wanted to marry, so I guess I'll just become a nun." And with that I flounced out of the room, already planning my escape.

WE WORKED OUT EVERY DETAIL. I was to meet Gene at the river bridge on the night of the full moon, and we were going to elope. I even practiced going down the stairs to see which ones squeaked. Gene talked to the sheriff, and Uncle Henry, who had informed him this might be a good idea, went with him. "Eileen is of legal age," the sheriff told Gene. I was nineteen and Gene was twenty. "And I trust you're not going to steal a car." Gene had bought his own pickup truck when he got out of the service.

Now the sheriff could have told my folks. Uncle Henry or Grandma could have told my folks what was up. Aunt Gladys and Uncle Ormond could have told my folks because they knew what was up, too. My brother John, who was seventeen by then, certainly could have told my folks if he wanted to make points and keep himself in the clear, but I knew Johnny would never tell on me. Or tell on Gene, for that matter; he adored Gene. Everybody adored Gene except my folks, and the only reason they didn't adore him is because they had blinders on about my future. "And because your dad doesn't want to lose his best sheepherder," said Gene. And I *was* his best herder too; I was the one who loved the sheep, and that made a difference in the herding. We went ahead with our plans.

That afternoon Uncle Henry had come down to the ranch, supposedly to see my dad, but really to let me know that this was the night for sure. Gene would be at the bridge waiting for me at midnight.

Of all nights, my parents picked this one to stay up late. Morning came at first light and there were the chores to do before any of us got started on the real work for the day. So we kids usually went to bed early and the folks did too, but they didn't go to sleep early on that most important night of my life. There was no paper delivery at the ranch and my dad loved to read the papers. As Grandma lived in town, she saved all the newspapers for him so he always picked them up in a bundle and read everything in them. Dad had been to Burns that day and picked up all the newspapers from Grandma, so he and Mom lay in bed until midnight reading by the gas light.

Finally, the folks turned off their light. I had the feeling that they were listening for me, because they didn't really trust me anymore. My brother went downstairs as if he were going to the outhouse. I had put my clothes in a flour sack, and I tiptoed to the window. When I saw John motion in the moonlight, I threw him the sack and he caught it before it even hit the ground. He carried the flour sack to the end of the haystack corral in the direction of the river bridge for me to pick up. Then he went over and let the air out of the tires on the folks' car. After that he came in and went to bed.

I waited for a while to leave, but I was afraid if I didn't get going pretty soon, Gene would think something had really gone wrong and would leave. Then I would really be in a mess. I slipped my pajamas on over my clothes and put my shoes on too. I left them untied the way I always did when I went to the outhouse at night but the strings seemed to be making a lot of noise as they dragged down the stairs. I lost count of which step I was on when I was fiddling with them and I couldn't remember which ones squeaked. Suddenly my brother said quietly, "Eileen, just walk," so I did.

I left my note on the table. "Don't be mad at me," the note read. "I've gone to get married."

Once out of the house I ran as fast as I could, picked up my flour sack of clothes, and cut across the field, jumping the windrows of hay that had just been mowed and not yet raked. The long stems were so slick that they shone like ice in the white moonlight. I fell several times. I thought of my horse Shamrock then and how we had fallen together when he jumped and how concerned he had been that I might have been hurt. Suddenly I got a hard lump in my chest. Was I leaving my entire life behind?

At last I could see the bridge across the river. There was Gene, sitting on the bridge waiting for me with his feet dangling above the water. He jumped up when he saw me and barely took time to kiss me before he threw my flour sack in the back of the pickup and we took off down the rough old dirt road as fast as we could go. We probably took ten years of life off Gene's pickup. When we got to the end of the levee road, we headed across the grease wood flats. There, parked in the dark, way off in the brush, was a dark colored car. The lights came on as soon as we went by.

✣

NEITHER GENE NOR I were habitual liars and we weren't used to sneaking around. Well, I was by now, I guess, because I'd been sneaking around with letters and seeing Gene ever since my folks had put the clamps on our relationship. But this kind of behavior wasn't natural for either one of us. When this car pulled out, we didn't try to get away; we froze like deer in the headlights.

Was this the sheriff going back on his word? Was it somehow my folks who had gotten wind of the plan? Or were these evil people thinking they could rob us for money? There were still robbers around, after all. Once when we were down in Fields, someone came over the southern pass of the Steens and broke into our house at the homestead. Dad caught the man, though, and broadcast a radio message to Burns for the sheriff. Dad was deputized to hold the robber so he had to stay up all night and guard him until the sheriff got to Fields. The man carried an iron in his pocket to knock out his victims, and he had been in the prison at Leavenworth twice before.

But it was none of the above. It was Uncle Ormond and Aunt Gladys, who were waiting to see if we made it or not. And as soon as we got onto the highway, there were more lights. Patrolling up and down the road was our high school friend, Harry Gouldin, who had a motorbike and was also wondering if we were going to get away. There was no other traffic and away we went, with Harry escorting us on his bike for ten miles before he turned around and went home.

Turns out that the folks had come after us, best they could. They heard me go out and heard the dogs bark at my unaccustomed behavior. Maybe Shamrock whinnied at me too, I don't know. When I didn't come back in, they came to look for me right away, and if Johnny hadn't let the air out of their tires, they would have caught me for sure. They drove that car with the air hissing out of the tires all the way to town and went straight to the sheriff's house and woke him up. He told them there was nothing that he could do because we were both of legal age so they might as well go back home. So, Dad said, surely the sheriff could at least arrest Gene for stealing that pickup. I would have thought the sheriff would have spared their feelings and not let on that he knew about the whole scheme, but he didn't. "Gene bought that pick up fair and square, and I have already talked to him, so go home and go to bed," he said.

WE DIDN'T FIND OUT ANY of this until later. We were headed across the high desert to Maupin where Gene's folks lived at the time. The next day we would go to The Dalles for a marriage license and then back to Oregon City, where we were married. But that night it was Gene and I traveling together in the bright white moonlight, driving across Oregon toward our new life.

✢

ALL THIS WAS SIXTY YEARS AGO, and Gene and I have been together ever since and have had a long and happy marriage. But there's something I have to get out of the way here and I wish I didn't have to tell it, but I guess I do. In real life people are much more complicated than any character that I ever could have created in my Ascripfa dreamland books as a child. This is about my dad, Steens Mountain Ben, a gentle man who loved his sheep and who never used his strength against others. Except once.

After Gene and I were married, we came back to Burns to live because Gene was working for Uncle Henry. When I think of it now it's rather amazing just how many available empty houses there were at that time on all the places that had been bought up by the bigger outfits. We weren't living very far from my folks but of course we didn't go over to see them; it was too soon to have anything to say. Besides, we were still in defiant mode, determined to show my folks and the rest of the world that we could make it on our own in spite of all the dire predictions for young lovers. Gene and I were lucky with several things going for us when we eloped. Gene had a job with my uncles and marketable skills as a mechanic and I had lots of training in the partnership of work. I worked for Uncle Henry too, cooking for the crews and driving the grain auger wherever it was needed for the harvest. We were young but we were ready for the challenges that marriage entails.

IT MUST HAVE BEEN ABOUT a month after we returned that we first ran into the folks. Even though they didn't go to town much, it was bound to happen sooner or later, and it happened at the carnival in Burns. Gene and I were going to splurge and go to the carnival and then take in a movie. It was almost time for the movie when we saw them coming down the street.

I guess my first impulse was to run, although in all honesty I can't say whether it was to run toward them or to run away. We just kept walking and I know I smiled a frozen kind of smile and Gene probably did too. None of us spoke until we were right together, just a few feet apart. When it happened, my mother turned instantly and ran toward their car.

Dad simply let loose with his fist and struck Gene in the face. There was no warning at all; Dad didn't say anything and he didn't wind up his arm, but suddenly he had hit Gene and the blood was flowing. Dad just stood there for a long minute as if to give Gene a chance to hit him back, but Gene never lifted his arms. Then Dad turned and walked toward his car where my mother was sitting with her hands over her face.

TO THIS DAY I DON'T KNOW exactly what Gene felt when that happened; my own feelings were so conflicted that I can't say for sure what I felt either, except I knew how much I loved them both and how sorry, sorry I was that this had happened. Gene and I went into the theater and I kept trying to put my handkerchief against his face but he just said, "I'm all right, I'm all right," and brushed it away.

I THOUGHT OF THE INCIDENT a lot that winter, but I didn't understand it then and it still seems terribly complicated. I see now that the one brief outburst of violence from my usually gentle father had more to it than just my dad's anger at Gene and me and the fact that we had, in a way, made a fool of him by having practically everyone else in Harney County helping us in our elopement. It was partly a timing issue.

I think I probably understood it the best when I went back several years later to see the old homestead house; it made me so sad to see the windows broken and the books Mom had left behind scattered on the floor she always kept so clean. My dad had been almost a hero to all who knew him on Steens Mountain; a man in control of his own place and family; a sheep man, not just a nomadic herder who worked for someone else or had to move from place to place on government land. To leave the Steens behind meant my mom and dad, through no fault of their own, had lost control of the dream of their youth. Although it surely worked out better financially for my folks in the long run to move from the mountain, I think of the dreams of the homesteaders every time we drive around eastern Oregon and I see weathered shacks in various stages of decay.

WE DIDN'T SEE THE FOLKS again until spring and that time Dad was pleasant, although a little stiff and formal. After that I got to going over to visit Mom, and things began to soften between us when they figured out a grandchild was coming. Probably my mom and all the girls in my high school class were counting the months, but Lora Kay wasn't born until a year after Gene and I were married. That really brought the folks around, as no one who loved kids like my dad was going to stay away from his first grandchild. Gene was perfectly gracious about the whole thing and even helped my dad mend his machinery whenever we went to see him. And my parents learned from their mistakes with me and treated my younger brother and sister differently.

AS I WATCHED MY OWN little girl grow, I thought often of the Steens. What was it that had made my life there so happy? Certainly not material things. Was it that I knew I was important in making a living for the family? Was it the courage and love between my parents that made me aspire to be like them? Was it the natural beauty of the mountains?

Or was it the life with the sheep? That I couldn't duplicate; even my father and mother, who by that time had bought their own ranch again down by Silver Lake, Oregon, had just sold the sheep and raised cattle exclusively. But my dad was sad about it and it showed in his poetry. "I sold my sheep, they are all gone…" his lament began. "No more will I the desert roam," he continued. "This era now is passing on." He understood it but he mourned for the way of life he had loved.

And I mourned for it too.

I HAVE BEEN a Steens Mountain child all my life.

Sometimes when I think about Steens Mountain, I think about it in smells: the smell of juniper, sage, wildflowers; the smell of the root cellar; the smell of Mom's cinnamon rolls baking or Dad's sourdough bread; the smell of the smoke from the little camp stove we used when we were herding the sheep. I can still get awfully lonesome for those smells, and now and then I can still get awfully lonesome for the Steens.

Afterword

Barbara J. Scot

WHEN MY NEIGHBOR Eileen O'Keeffe McVicker told me that she had been trying to write about her childhood on Steens Mountain for thirty years, I was not surprised by her tenacity. I was already in awe of Eileen, an octogenarian who reaped a bountiful harvest from her acreage and kept a large workshop in which she pursued a variety of arts and craft projects with seemingly unlimited zeal. All this creative energy, she assured me, was due to her high desert background on the family homestead in southeastern Oregon: a hard, happy life, much of it spent outdoors, herding her father's sheep.

I loved the magnificent Steens with its adjacent wildlife refuge, so I asked if I could read her stories. She would share what she had written, she promised, after she polished it up a bit. But Eileen's stories wouldn't polish to her satisfaction; a year after I had requested them, she e-mailed me and asked for help in putting something together that would have a chance for publication. So our collaboration began.

Initially I was overwhelmed by the scattered entries of Eileen's green notebook. Memory is kaleidoscopic, not linear, and her collection was more of a collage than a narrative. The overlapping episodic fragments did not offer easy potential for publication in an industry that still prefers an identifiable story arc in nonfiction as well as fiction: a beginning, middle, and end. Her written anecdotes, though interspersed with occasional poetic phrases, were abbreviated and devoid of details. Even before I finished the first reading, however, the unique niche her childhood occupied in the history of Western homesteading was apparent. Sheepherding and Steens Mountain: Eileen had a story to tell, and I was being offered a rare privilege to share in the telling. A phrase reached out to me. *I was an outdoor child all my life.*

That line was the portal by which I entered her world; I, too, was an outdoor child, reared in a rural environment among animals and nature, and I had written about it. Perhaps, by encouraging Eileen to supply description and to flesh out the written accounts of her adventures I could help, after all. I committed that line to paper, searched through the notebook for related phrases, composed a few transitions, and then e-mailed her the first narrative paragraphs.

"Does this sound like you?" I asked.

"Yes," Eileen replied. "That sounds right."

Next I began e-mailing specific questions generated by her abbreviated accounts. These Eileen answered with much greater detail in the e-mails than she had supplied in the original written version; sometimes the new telling spawned another story entirely. This informal medium seemed particularly liberating for Eileen's writing, and she provided long passages I could use verbatim. "More about your mother, please," evoked a wonderful description of the ingenuity demanded of women in the harsh homesteading environment—women who shared in all the outside labor but changed back into their frocks when serving meals, women who during this transitional period of the early twentieth century had to be able to cope with both horses and automobiles. "My mom could take a car where most people wouldn't take a horse," Eileen stated with pride. We began waking in the middle of the night, only to find our correspondence had crossed. This midnight mode of exchange energized us and we supplemented it with face-to-face conversations. A narrative that satisfied both Eileen and me began to emerge.

In these days of "truth-in-memoirs" it seems necessary to delineate for both publishers and readers exactly how much of this narrative is Eileen O'Keeffe McVicker and how much is Barbara J. Scot, especially as the story is told in first person. As a general statement I can say that the episodes are mostly in Eileen's words, albeit much rearranged from successive accounts with necessary transitions, and the organization is mine. The most demonstrable example of Eileen's exact wording occurs in the episodes like the Honey Bunch stories, which Eileen provided in three different mediums: her original notebook, her e-mails, and oral conversation. This multilayered account of basically the same material gave me the best preparation for assuming her actual voice. In all of the narrative, however, Eileen's facts became my facts, her people became my people, and her language became my language. In several instances, especially in Part Two, I encouraged her to reflect on her feelings surrounding a particular incident. She would do so in conversation or written e-mails, and I would include what she said. But I did not create this story; Eileen lived it.

Eileen not only lived this adventurous life, she looked back at it with a fierce love for family, Steens Mountain, and sheep that led her to emphasize the positive aspect of every experience and minimize her own and her parents' hardships. Consider her description of being sent to far pastures to check for new lambs: her legs were tired ("in those days children didn't complain"), coyote calls echoed between the hills, she was conscious of the threat from feral bulls and rattlesnakes and the gathering darkness. "When you are a child and walking a long way from home, every little thing seems a danger," Eileen observed with characteristic understatement of the courage required to carry out her assigned task.

We needed a progressive story line that moved us through Eileen's anecdotal collection. The beginning of Eileen's story was easy; all the time on the mountain that developed Eileen's deep love of nature, the rhythm of life with sheep that followed the ancient transhumant practice of grazing on higher pastures as the seasons progressed. As a former teacher I kept thinking that Eileen's stories would be invaluable in a social studies class, especially integrated with assignments on Native American use of Steens Mountain, early range wars, or evolving environmental attitudes. The O'Keeffes provided a veritable case study of the brief homesteading period in the arid West, with Eileen's childhood a fascinating model of how children develop confidence to face challenges creatively.

We trailed with the sheep to the Greenhouse Ranch south of Burns, and the adolescent Eileen tackled all situations with the determined ingenuity she had learned from her childhood on Steens Mountain.

Unexpectedly she handed me the means to move beyond our anecdotal clusters of memories into a more active story line. When the picture of a spirited bay horse that hung in her hallway caught my eye, she gave me the story of Shamrock and Gene. None of this had been included in her original notebook, but she outlined it in an e-mail that night and I pursued the story relentlessly in conversation. With that as a framework we were able to move from the specific early twentieth century story of sheepherding and homesteading to the more universal saga of the separation process faced by parents and their children in every time and place.

The ending was more elusive. Editor Tom Booth at Oregon State University Press confirmed in a phone call my own sentiment that the desert drive into the eastern Oregon moonrise I had originally used to conclude the action did not have quite the finality that the entire account required. So back I went to Eileen's dining table and over a cup of coffee I repeated the conversation I'd had with the editor, citing our mutual feeling that we needed a more satisfying close to the narrative. What happened, I questioned, the first time she saw her parents after she returned from that moonlight flight? I had asked that question before, but this time, somewhat reluctantly, she gave a much more complete account, which precipitated the most frustrating moment of our collaboration. I recognized immediately that we had the perfect incident to tie the experience of the O'Keeffes to the disappointed dreams of other homesteaders. Feeling that the story reflected negatively on her father, Eileen didn't want to include it, and she had the final call. This was, after all, her life we were recording, and I had submitted every page of the manuscript for her approval.

I went home, wrote up what Eileen had told me, and e-mailed it to Tom Booth at OSU Press. Here's the ending, I wrote, but she doesn't want me to use it. He composed a thoughtful response. This episode, he said, again confirming my own sentiments, in no way diminishes the participants; in fact, it humanizes them and provides exactly the needed closure for the narrative. So I pasted together an e-mail to Eileen. I explained that I had been personally so moved by the incident she described that I felt a responsibility to respond to the editorial direction I had been given. I copied both the alternate ending and Tom Booth's response and I sent her the whole thing. If she would at least read this and reconsider, I would promise to abide by her decision. I meant that, but I admit that I waited anxiously for her answer.

I waited all day with increased nervousness that I had violated our easy working relationship with my visceral response to what she had given me in trust. She usually answered my e-mails quickly. Surely she must be considering how to formulate her negative reply, I thought unhappily, but it turned out that she had simply been gone all day on errands. At midnight I finally got her measured e-mail. She liked the way I had told the story, she said, and she saw what the editor meant. After reading everything through twice, once aloud to her husband, she decided I could use the story.

A FEW MONTHS AFTER we had finished the manuscript, Eileen and I visited the homestead site together. A range fire that burned over the southern pass several years ago left only a few scattered remnants of the O'Keeffe homestead to show anyone had lived there, ever. Except for a dark green patch of reeds and the rhubarb plant that Eileen's grandmother had brought with her from Crane in 1930, the hillside was all late summer colors: blond cheat grass and September shades of dusty yellow sage. "The garden was well behind the house," Eileen told me, pointing uphill at the rhubarb. "It seemed farther away when I was a little girl. The better spring is way down there where the reservoir still holds water." She waved at a larger stand of reeds approximately a quarter of a mile away that rippled against the blue backdrop of the Pueblo range of mountains. "That's where we went for water every day and on that hillside is where my dad had that run-in with the rabid coyote."

Still higher on the hill-of-the-rabid-coyote, a jagged tooth of rimrock poked through the ridgeline. "That's the Big Seat. Grandma and I climbed up there many times to find wildflowers and to watch the sunrise." Together we crossed a hard pan of clay where not even the sagebrush grew. "I was running barefoot when I stepped on a rattle-snake that was gliding across this spot. I just kept on going as the snake slid under my foot. It was like running on marbles." Continuing down-hill we came to where a broken rusty stove lay on its side. A strand of willow fence-weave from the corral. A broken cup with a familiar pattern. A lid from one of the water-tight kettles that had been cooled in the stream at summer sheep camp. Eileen picked up something here, something there and reconstructed her childhood, tying each fragment to a story that we had included in the narrative of *Child of Steens Mountain*.

In spite of the soft, blue curves of the Pueblos and the sweep of shadows on the sloped rise to the high mesa she called the Rincon, the whole place seemed stark and desert lonesome to me, and Eileen knew it. "I wish there was more left of the place for you to see," she said, sensing that I wasn't feeling the same poetry of place that she had felt as a child while watching the sheep. She needn't have worried; I knew from writing my own memoirs the difficulty of transmitting the beauty of one's childhood to others. "I try to come every year," she said, sounding more matter-of-fact than sentimental. Dust devils danced in the hot September wind.

THE DAY AFTER EILEEN AND I visited the homestead site, I drove the Steens Mountain Loop, the highest road in Oregon, which goes clear to the windy summit. I did not expect to encounter any sheep. The western side of this large fault-block mountain slides upward in such a deceptive, friendly slope that the glacier-carved gorges that drop away through jagged lava pillars at the higher elevations are always a rugged surprise. The aspens were just beginning to turn gold in the meadows. A sage hen scuttled across the road. I was looking for a place on the mountain with the colorful name of Whorehouse Meadows, a designation that had been given because of the activities practiced there during the early 1920s when some enterprising women sensed a summer market from lonesome herders. Eileen had never mentioned this. They had lived on the other end of the mountain, and if her parents had censored the comics that hunters had brought for their children, they likely wouldn't have told them this story when they were young. The guidebook said it was about a mile and a half above Fish Lake at approximately eight thousand feet elevation in an aspen grove, and I must have been almost at that point when I saw the sheep. I forgot completely about Whorehouse Meadows and its traveling bordello.

Although I was quite far away from them, I knew they were sheep, these white dots moving slowly across a lake that was all dried up now with still-green grass in the shallow bed. The lead sheep continued grazing up the slope onto a lava slab that looked to me like solid rock with no vegetation. I parked the car by the side of the road and walked through sagebrush and rocky gullies. Were there rattlesnakes at high elevations this late in the season? I needed Eileen and her trusty bush-beating stick with me.

The sheep had all moved slightly uphill from the dry lake bed. I didn't see the herder or his dogs, so I sat down on a rock. For just one moment I wanted to celebrate the joyful way of life that Eileen had experienced as a child; a traditional existence in harmony with seasonal cycles, lived mostly outdoors in the beauty of nature. I was close enough now to hear the bells of the sheep and their soft contrapuntal conversation as they grazed leisurely up the dark slope. The bowl shape of the hillsides around the lake bed made an echo of these melded sounds, like someone was whispering to a musical accompaniment. No wonder Idaho folklorist Louie Attebery had chosen a Bach chorale, "Sheep May Safely Graze," as the title for his work about sheep and the families who followed them to higher pastures through the endless cycles of seasons and life. I truly felt it then, the beauty that Eileen had wanted me to feel at the homestead site, the magic of her childhood on the mountain and the poetry of sheep. What a gift I had been given to share in the telling of this story.

THIS WRITING EXPERIENCE IN autobiography is not for every author; it requires an honest reverence for another's life experience, an iron grip on one's own choice of language, and a certain surrender of literary freedom. In this case, however, I was profoundly rewarded. For the few months I was privileged to write in Eileen O'Keeffe McVicker's voice, I, too, became a Steens Mountain child. I saw wild horses on the distant rimrock. I smelled the early morning sunshine of the mountain, and I felt the distant warmth of other herders' campfires as evening descended on the sheep.

Acknowledgments

I WISH TO THANK EVERYONE who has helped me with *Child of Steens Mountain*, including Tom Booth and Micki Reaman at Oregon State University Press for their belief in the book; Molly Gloss and Bob Boyd for their reviews of the original manuscript; Richard Etulain and Barbara J. Scot for the Foreword and Afterword, respectively; Elizabeth Quinn and Thomas Osborne for publishing an excerpt in *High Desert Journal*; and so many many more. Thank you to my husband Gene for all his patience waiting for me to finish whatever it was I writing so we could go do something or head off somewhere. Thanks to my daughter Lora, son-in-law Ron, grandchildren Kim and Rogan, and to the family and friends who have cheered me on. Thanks, too, to Teddy and Judy, friends from grade school, for talking over all that happened. And to my cousin Pauline for her pushing!

And special thanks to the wonderful, beautiful, and hard-working Barbara Scot! Without Barbara, this book would never have happened. I was writing stories and more stories, with the idea that my notebook would someday end up on a shelf. Maybe my family would enjoy the stories; in the far back of my mind I imagined that someday it might actually get published. Well, Barbara saw to that!

Many thanks to all for making an eighty-year-old lady's dream come true!

—Eileen O'Keeffe McVicker

IN ADDITION TO Eileen McVicker's acknowledgments, Barbara Scot wishes to thank the following: Charles Cannon (Professor Emeritus, Coe College, Cedar Rapids, Iowa) for his careful reading, editorial comments, and forty years of faith in my writing.

Mark Highberger of Bear Creek Press, author and publisher of many books of western history, for his recognition of the value of Eileen's story and helpful suggestions.

Several friends for reading early drafts and offering encouragement: Mary Forst, Sheilah Toomey, Clair Hekker, Barbara LaMorticella, Patty Denny, Beth Sparks, Susie Walsleben, Judy Wilder, Nancy Schlunz, Eloise Helgens, and Violet Murphy.

And special thanks to my husband Jim Trusky for his endurance and support.

EILEEN O'KEEFFE MCVICKER and BARBARA J. SCOT are neighbors on Sauvie Island, north of Portland, Oregon, who met while walking their dogs.

McVicker, born near Fields, Oregon, in 1927, lives on an acreage with fruit trees and a large shop where she and her husband practice several arts and crafts in an active retirement. They also have a house in Burns, Oregon, where they spend time in the summer.

Scot, a public school teacher for twenty-five years, began to write after a tour with the Peace Corps in Nepal in 1991. She has published three books: *The Violet Shyness of Their Eyes: Notes from Nepal* (winner of the PNBA Book Award); *Prairie Reunion* (*New York Times* Notable Book of the Year); and *The Stations of Still Creek*. An avid fan of the outdoors, she has spent much of her life climbing mountains, backpacking, running, and bird watching. She and her husband live in a houseboat on the Willamette River.

RICHARD W. ETULAIN is professor emeritus of history and formerly director of the Center for the American West at the University of New Mexico, where he taught from 1979 until retirement in 2001. He is the author or editor of more than forty books, most of which focus on the history and literature of the American West. They include *Conversations with Wallace Stegner on Western History and Literature* and *Beyond the Missouri: The Story of the American West*.